WINING AND DINING
IN FRANCE

Other books by Robin Neillands include

Walking through France – from the Channel to the Camargue (Collins)
Cycletouring in France (Oxford Illustrated Press)
The Road to Compostela (Moorland)
Classic Walks in France (with David Wickers) (Oxford Illustrated Press)
Walking in France (Oxford Illustrated Press)
The Hundred Years War (Routledge, Chapman & Hall)
History, People & Places in Burgundy (Spurbooks)
The French Pyrenees (Spurbooks)
A Visitor's Guide to Brittany (Moorland)
A Visitor's Guide to the Dordogne (Moorland)

WINING AND DINING IN FRANCE

in
Association with the
Logis et Auberges de France

Robin Neillands

ASHFORD, BUCHAN & ENRIGHT
Southampton

Published in 1990 by Ashford, Buchan & Enright Ltd,
1 Church Road, Shedfield, Hampshire SO3 2HW

British Library Cataloguing in Publication Data

Neillands, Robin, *1935–*
    The Ashford guide to wining & dining in France.
    1. France. Food & drink
    I. Title
    641'.0944

    ISBN 1-85253-173-8

Typeset by Acorn Bookwork, Salisbury, Wiltshire
Printed in Great Britain

While great care has been taken in the compilation of this book, the
author and publisher cannot guarantee that all details, such as
prices, schedules, addresses and telephone numbers will remain
unchanged and exactly as quoted here.
    The author has no connection with any business or
establishment cited here, and no guarantee or endorsement is
implied or given in this respect. That a business or establishment is
not listed or detailed does not imply any criticism.

CONTENTS

PHOTOGRAPHS

ACKNOWLEDGEMENTS

Thanks are due to Renée Payoux of the *Logis et Auberges de France*; Patrick Goyet and Pauline Hallam of the French Government Tourist Office in London; Sue Ockwell of VFB Holidays; Richard and Linda Hearn of Inntravel, Helmsley, York; Toby Oliver of the Brittany Ferries Information Bureau; Jane Whigham and Christopher Bramwell for their exploration of the Lot; Eve Livet of Lyon; Chantal Larinier of Paris; and many – too many to mention – hoteliers and restaurateurs of France.

Robin Neillands
St-Nicolas-de-Bourgeuil
Loire (August 1989)

A MESSAGE FROM THE PRESIDENT OF *LES LOGIS ET AUBERGES DE FRANCE*

France has much to offer the traveller, not least the gastronomic pleasures that form so large a part of French life. These pleasures can be found at everyday meals or on grand occasions, in the most prestigious restaurants or in quite modest establishments.

The hoteliers of the *Logis et Auberges de France* have this French gastronomic tradition very much to heart and aim to offer good value, combined with the rich and authentic cookery traditional to their own regions. The reader will readily understand how the many references to the *Logis* hotels in this book are here simply because most feature in particular the local wines and dishes of their region.

The *Logis* are particularly well placed to provide information about local food and wine – our membership of 5000 country hotels stages a Regional Cookery Contest every year, in which the competitors discover, or rediscover, the variety of dishes they can offer to their guests, some from ancient recipes, others newly created by our chefs, but all based on fresh local produce.

We in the *Logis et Auberges de France* offer comfortable accommodation in a great variety of family-run hotels, but we also offer good food at no great cost, and excellent value for money at every level. I therefore wish this book every success, and am sure that by using it, the traveller in France will discover the pleasures that fine local cooking can bring to the body and the mind.

Louis Heilmann
President
Les Logis et Auberges de France

INTRODUCTION

Wining and dining on good food and wine in pleasant surroundings is both one of the great joys of civilization and one of life's simpler pleasures. It remains a highly subjective experience, so the first point I must make in this book is that the pleasures and prejudices concerning food, wine and restaurants expressed in this book are always personal and largely mine, albeit backed by those of many like-minded friends. Furthermore, to give this book that professional touch I have relied on the judgement and skill of many French chefs working in that most excellent hotel consortium, the *Logis et Auberges de France*, who sent in their menus and suggestions. If my tastes in food and wine broadly coincide with your own, this book will have a great deal to offer you on your own travels through the provinces of France.

However, I am not a food writer, well versed in arcane cooking skills, or a wine writer with years of prime wines at my fingertips. I am a travel writer, and I rate eating out in France as one of the great bonuses of travelling in that delightful country. Even so, I think it is valid to approach the subject from the diner's point of view, considering the end rather than the means, the quality of the dish rather than the details of the recipe, but let me make it clear that this book is *not* about French food. Rather, it is an introduction to the pleasures of dining in the varied provinces of France, where the local sights are a back-drop to the dishes. To this end the book includes a list of some five hundred provincial hotels and restaurants where, on current evidence, one can dine well, and at no great expense, especially on local dishes.

As I could never have compiled this book *and* eaten my way through five hundred meals in the space of a single year, I enlisted the support of fellow diners with similar tastes, charging them to provide me with details of any restaurant where they ate well, in a pleasant atmosphere and at a price which represented good value for money. This approach has brought to light many of the places recommended in this book, and since I travel indefatigably in France I supplemented their experiences with my own, gathered in recent visits for, alas, restaurants do change, and not always for the better.

It was then drawn to my attention that the *Logis et Auberges de France*, which currently numbers some five thousand privately owned country hotels among its membership, holds an annual Regional Cookery Contest, with prizes for every stage from local to national level. Like many travellers in France, I have long admired the hotels of the *Logis* network, so I contacted their headquarters and suggested that this book might be a means of bringing the entrants in their competition and the standard of French country cooking to the attention of a wider audience. The organization adopted this suggestion and menus began to flow into my office.

There are two main reasons for enlisting the help of the *Logis et Auberges de France*. Quite apart from enabling me to include more good places, it gives some assurance of lasting quality. Any chef willing to submit his work to the judgement of his peers and neighbours must care about his food and maintain high standards. This is doubly important in a book aimed at the British market, because it has sometimes been felt that an influx of British diners to a French restaurant often leads to a decline in the quality of the food and a hike in the prices. (Most Francophile travellers would agree that the two most off-putting sights outside a French restaurant are a host of metal plaques around the door and a mass of GB plates in the carpark.)

I therefore felt I needed to find chefs who would stand up to the indifference of the passing clientele, and the subsequent temptation to reduce standards. A competitor in a national cookery competition seems likely to resist such pressure, and will appreciate the fact that most of the entries in this book are restaurants in country hotels, where the foreign visitors usually arrive in the summer. Any chef who lets his standards slip in the summer may find the locals unwilling to return to his restaurant in the winter.

I have talked to scores, maybe hundreds, of French chefs over the last two years and without exception they tell me that the thing which keeps them on their toes and makes their work worthwhile is the response of the clientele. The work of a professional chef demands long hours, starting with a visit to the market early in the morning and going on until the kitchen is clean and quiet again about midnight. An 18-hour day is quite common. If the result of this is indifference at the sharp end, a request for more chips and stewed cabbage, then the chef's commitment inevitably declines. I once visited a hotel in the Cotentin Peninsula, in Normandy, and found that while the situation was perfect and the staff pleasant, the food was little short of disgusting. I therefore sought out the owner and told him so, but he took the wind out of my sails completely by agreeing with me. 'We can cook good food, M'sieu, but your countrymen won't eat it . . . they like a full plate and don't care about the quality . . . it's very sad.' Eyes opened, I returned to the dining room and saw what he meant. There, elbows out and forks flashing, my countrymen were hoovering down the slop, with evident enjoyment.

Personally speaking, I do not like *nouvelle cuisine*. The best definition of that arty kind of cooking came from a friend of mine who declared that after a full meal of *nouvelle cuisine*, he had to rush home for a bacon sandwich. On the other hand I do not care for stodge. On the cost front, I think if caviar was 50p the pound, no one would eat it. I don't like entrails, blood or brains, although I include those who do among my helpers, and since one has to be fair, there are *nouvelle cuisine* restaurants listed in this book – but not many.

On the positive side I like soups and stews and 'made dishes', pies and puddings. I like fish without bones and meat without heavy sauces. I think the quality of a restaurant is often best judged from the vegetables. I like, in short, good, traditional, flavoursome meals, cooked with skill and served pleasantly and without pretence. I feel the current elevation of panhandlers to celebrity status is ridiculous and an insult to many hard-working people who manage to serve good food day after day without becoming pretentious or charging the earth for it. I believe in value for money. I prefer cheese to puddings and Armagnac to Cognac. I like small, personally-run restaurants, which smell wonderful the minute you open the door.

Clearly, I could go on and on sharpening my personal axe before setting out to cut down the forest of claptrap which surrounds the necessary business of eating and drinking. Let me hold back and say that if wining and dining is listed among your personal pleasures, then we have something in common. In the hope that we can proceed from that point to our mutual enjoyment, let me tell you more about this book.

The book takes its structure from the regions used by the *Logis et Auberges de France*. The description of each region begins with an outline of its touristic attractions, and a suggested touring route round most of them. Those who wish to make their own way around might still find the check-list of Essential Sights useful. These are included not only for their intrinsic interest, but also because many of the hotels and restaurants lie on or close to them, in many cases on roads which foreign visitors to these parts are likely to follow. It seems reasonable to assume that anyone visiting, say, Normandy, is more likely to visit Rouen, Honfleur, Caen and the D-Day beaches, places with historical appeal, than make directly for, say, Alençon, or some village in the Alpes-Mancelles.

This tourist information is followed by short sections on the local food and wine, if any, with some mention of local dishes which may appear on local menus and in particular on those of *Logis et Auberges de France* hotel-restaurants serving regional cuisine. Finally, there comes a list of restaurants and *Logis* hotel-restaurants in that particular region or province, selected from those encountered on my travels or the travels of my friends or from the contestants in the *Logis et Auberges de France* Cookery Competition.

A word of caution: no guarantees are given here that the delights experienced on our visits will be repeated on yours. Our tastes may simply not be the same. But that apart, cooks have days off and off-days, restaurants change hands, standards rise and fall. Even so, there is a very strong probability that you too will enjoy a good or very good French meal and get value for money in any of the restaurants listed. *Bon appétit!*

About the French

One of the constant tasks of any Francophile is to justify a liking for the French. Being a fairly vocal Francophile I hear horror stories all the time, of rudeness and arrogance and downright chicanery, and a sad tale it all is. I can only say for my part that I don't find the French like that at all. I find them ranging from the coolly polite to the warmly hospitable and my overall impression is that if you go halfway to meet the French, they will come more than halfway in return. Nevertheless, 'Love France – can't stand the French' is an all-too-common attitude, which seems to me a pity.

The fact is that the French are in some ways very different from the British, but in many ways the same. Both peoples are reserved and terrible at languages. I find that among older people it is the English who speak a little French, and among the younger, the French who speak a little English. The French tend to be formal, so the British must break the ice and in this a smile helps. Most French people, even Parisian taxi drivers, will buckle at the knees if you give them a great big smile – try it. It also helps if you speak a little French – even a few phrases will help. On entering a restaurant, for example, a nod and a muttered 'M'sieur . . . Mesdames' to the assembled throng, will go down well, and a 'Bon appétit' to the nearest table will not go amiss either.

Above all, it is worth remembering that wining and dining in France is a serious business. I cannot recall seeing one of those raucous parties that are all too common nowadays in British restaurants, one table keeping the entire place in uproar. The best way to get on with the French is to acknowledge the fact that you are in their country and act accordingly. Besides, it's more fun that way.

About the *Logis et Auberges de France*

Since this book lists mainly *Logis et Auberges de France* establishments, it might be helpful to say more about the organization itself. It is an hotel consortium, founded in 1949 to bring together and promote the services of the better-run, privately owned country hotels of France. The country aspect is worth stressing, because there are no *Logis* hotels in Paris, and very few in the large towns. Therefore Paris does not feature in this book, and I have had to recommend non-*Logis* restaurants for some of the large provincial towns. There are currently 4015 *Logis* hotels, classified as 1- or 2-star tourist hotels, and 533 *Auberges*, which are hotels with too few rooms to qualify for star ratings. By the time this book appears, the membership will top 5000. Membership of the *Logis* network requires the hotel to give (1) a warm welcome to the paying guest; (2) offer comfortable accommodation in accordance with its designation; (3) offer a menu or menus which feature regional dishes as well as the chef's own specialities; and (4) offer prices inclusive of service.

Logis do vary, but what they have in common – if this is not a contradiction in terms – is individuality. This can mean that the visitor encounters eccentricity, but since the people who run the hotel also own it, they have a vested interest in running it well. The annual *Guide des Hôtels-restaurants, Logis et Auberges de France*, which lists all the establishments currently in the consortium, is one book that should be on the bookshelf of every traveller to France. It is available free from the French Government Tourist Office in London. I have used the *Logis* network extensively while travelling in France and I recommend it to you.

Hotels and restaurants

France plays host to the great international hotels, the Hiltons and Sheratons, and apart from internal hotel chains of its own, also has famous hotels, such as the George V in Paris and the Négresco in Nice. This book, however, is largely concerned with small hotels, and few of them lie in large cities. I have chosen hotels with good restaurants, plus some other restaurants, either in big cities where you may stop for lunch, or in places where, for some reason, there is no *Logis* hotel. In the main though, the restaurants in this book are in hotels and in the course of assembling a list of them, a few points caught my eye.

First, the better food tends to be in the smaller hotels. You are more likely to get a good meal in a 10-room country hotel than in a 50-room one – probably because the restaurant is more important in the small hotel. Secondly, my study of menu prices suggests that you get what you pay for. Good food is hardly possible at F40 (say £4) for three courses. Most of the restaurants in this book have menus priced from F75 to F150 or a little higher, and for those prices you will get value for money in sound, well-prepared food.

As always, when booking a room or a table, it pays to make arrangements in advance. The simplest way to do this is by telephone. When calling from the UK, dial: 010 for an Overseas line; 33 for France; and then the number. For example, for Madame Menendez' Hôtel des Pyrénées in Ax-les-Thermes you would dial 010-33, then the *départemental* code (61) and then the number 64-21-01; that is, 010-33-61-64-21-01. You then have to book the room or the table. It is worth asking if the respondent speaks English: 'Parlez-vous anglais, Madame/Monsieur?' If not, since the respondent is well aware of your reason for ringing, say, 'J'ai besoin d'une chambre pour deux personnes pour la nuit du huit Janvier.' This, freely translated means, 'I need a double room for the night of 8 January.' If you want a double bed, ask for a *grand lit* – and when you get there, the pillows are in the wardrobe. I am not going to stud this book with useful French phrases, but I recommend you acquire a good dictionary and a reliable phrase book. One of the snags with asking set, stereotyped questions is that they lead the listener to think you know more French than you do, and you will then be deluged with French in reply. Asking the question is only half the battle – you also have to understand the answer.

When roaming through France it is not usually necessary to book ahead outside the holiday month of August, though beware of *le Départ*, the holiday weekend at the end of July, when it seems that all France takes to the road. Your existing hotel will usually be happy to ring ahead and book a room for you in case of doubt. When you arrive, or are attempting to find a room, the receptionist will probably ask, 'Vous dînez ici?' and if you say no, the room may be suddenly unavailable. It is anyway quite a good idea to dine in the hotel restaurant and those listed in this book are usually very good.

Eating in France

Breakfast in France is usually charged separately and can be relatively expensive – say F80 for the room but F20 for the coffee and croissants with butter and jam. All such prices are displayed behind the bedroom door incidentally, so you know where you are. If you want an egg or an orange juice they will be charged as an extra.

Lunch is normally between 12 and 2 pm. However, certainly in the countryside, it may be difficult to find a meal after 1.30 pm, although they tend to eat lunch and dinner later the further south you go. My advice is to get into the restaurant at lunchtime between 12.30 and 1 pm, and in the evening be ready to dine by 7.30 pm. Prices are displayed outside the restaurants and there is usually a choice of either fixed *menus* at various prices from F45 up, plus a more or less extensive *carte*. Some of the smaller restaurants offer wine-inclusive menus, and you may even find a big bottle of *rouge* already on the table. Otherwise you order a bottle in the usual way, or try the *vin de maison*, which may come in a small jug (*pichet*), or, in Brittany and Normandy, perhaps cider (*cidre*). If you want water there will be Vittel or Perrier or a jug filled from the kitchen tap, *l'eau plat* – flat water. I have always found French tap water perfectly safe to drink.

The menus are a set selection of dishes at a price which includes tax and service. There will usually be a selection, a simple *prix fixe*, the standard set meal, then a higher priced one, then a *menu touristique*, and maybe a *menu gastronomique*. Eating from a menu, you do not have to have every course, but you may well be charged for the ones you miss out. Anything extra or off the *carte* will be charged as a supplement, although I have often found that the restaurateur is quite happy to substitute a dish from another menu or even from the *carte* at no extra charge. Having studied the menu and made your choice, up comes the waiter or waitress, to take the order. If you have chosen you then order, and since many British restaurants give their menus in French I foresee no difficulty here. The only possible snags are over meat, where you will have to specify *bleu* (rare) or *à point* (medium). Medium is about as far as the French usually go, but if you like your steak well cooked ask for *bien cuit* (well done) or even *brûlé* (burnt). Salads are often served as a separate course.

Cheese comes before the pudding, not after it as in Britain, and the coffee is extra. Finally, ask for the bill: 'L'addition, s'il vous plaît.' If the service is included there is no need to leave a tip.

Wine

The wine list – *la carte du vin* – will likewise present few problems to those who already enjoy eating out at home. If we put the great vintages and châteaux wines on one side for the moment, then in declining order of merit – and usually price – wines are graded AC (*Appellation Contrôlée*) or AOC (*Appellation d'Origine Contrôlée*). These wines are nationally recognized and quality controlled to ensure that they come from a defined region, are produced from certain types of grapes grown in a particular way, and are available only in limited, though often generous, amounts. AC–AOC are, in short, the first-quality wines, though the vintages do vary. VDQS (*Vins Délimités de Qualité Supérieure*) wines are also carefully controlled, though to lower standards than those demanded of AC or AOC producers. Then come the *vins de pays*, which bear the names of the regions they come from. If you want a local wine you ask for a *vin de la région*, and finally *vins de table*, which can also cover the *vins de pays* and everything not AC or VDQS. A small tip: one restaurateur told me that his *worst* drinking wine was not the cheapest, but the cheapest but one. 'People do not like to order the cheapest wine on the list – they always go for the one above, so that is where I put the wine which is, well, not so good.' In this book I have tried to recommend that you try the local wines wherever possible. They are often very suited to the local food, and usually cheaper than more famous names, so unless you have a very refined palate, you will often find local wines an excellent choice.

THE REGIONS OF FRANCE

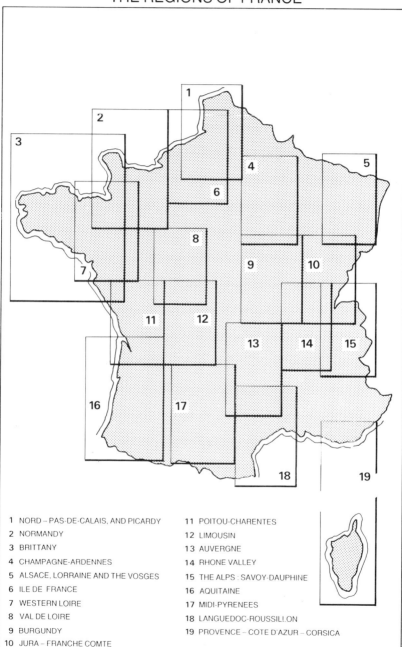

1 NORD – PAS-DE-CALAIS, AND PICARDY
2 NORMANDY
3 BRITTANY
4 CHAMPAGNE-ARDENNES
5 ALSACE, LORRAINE AND THE VOSGES
6 ILE DE FRANCE
7 WESTERN LOIRE
8 VAL DE LOIRE
9 BURGUNDY
10 JURA – FRANCHE COMTE

11 POITOU-CHARENTES
12 LIMOUSIN
13 AUVERGNE
14 RHONE VALLEY
15 THE ALPS : SAVOY-DAUPHINE
16 AQUITAINE
17 MIDI-PYRENEES
18 LANGUEDOC-ROUSSILLON
19 PROVENCE – COTE D'AZUR – CORSICA

NORD – PAS-DE-CALAIS, AND PICARDY

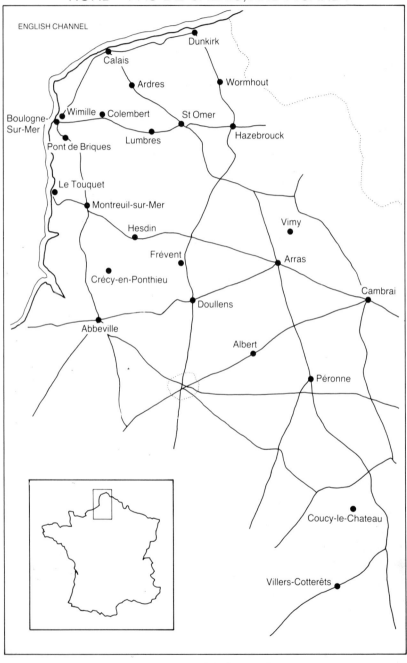

ENGLISH CHANNEL

Dunkirk
Calais
Ardres
Wormhout
Boulogne-Sur-Mer
Wimille
Colembert
St Omer
Hazebrouck
Pont de Briques
Lumbres
Le Touquet
Montreuil-sur-Mer
Hesdin
Vimy
Frévent
Arras
Crécy-en-Ponthieu
Cambrai
Doullens
Abbeville
Albert
Péronne
Coucy-le-Chateau
Villers-Cotterêts

NORD
PAS-DE-CALAIS
AND PICARDY

Although the two regions of northern France, Nord – Pas-de-Calais, and Picardy, are separate areas, they can be considered together here for convenience and because they have strong historic links. In medieval times they formed part of the Dukedom of Burgundy, and more recently were the ravaged battlefields of the Great War. For the British visitor, these parts of France are worthy of further study. Although the weather can be dreary, and the eastern parts of once-industrial Artois are still scarred by coalmines, there is a great deal of historic interest, as well as a notable local cuisine and some very fine restaurants. Certainly, lovers of good French food will find it here in abundance – if they shop around.

There is also the advantage of proximity, at least for the visitor from the south-east of England. Every part of these two regions lies within easy reach of the short-haul Channel ports of Dunkirk (Dunquerque), Calais and Boulogne, and will grow nearer yet when the Channel Tunnel opens. The area is ideal for weekend visits, shopping expeditions and gastronomic forays. Some will also consider it an advantage that, because more visitors stream south for Paris or sunnier climes, the region has not been overrun by tourism.

The two regions total four *départements*: Nord – Pas de Calais comprises just two, Nord and Pas-de-Calais, while the ancient province of Picardy adds Aisne and the fatal Somme, since the Oise *département* more properly belongs to the Ile de France, the region around Paris. To gain an historical overview of this part of France, one might begin in the town of Calais, which was captured from the French by King Edward III in 1347 and remained English until 1558. A famous bronze statue, *The Burghers of Calais*, stands before the Calais Cloth Hall and recalls one event in the siege in 1347, when Edward III was about to hang the senior citizens of the town and was dissuaded from doing so by Queen Philippa. Look around the outskirts of Calais and you will find that remnants of old ramparts, many from the seventeenth and eighteenth centuries, can still be found among the newer buildings and industrial estates of this thriving town and busy port. This historical snippet is relevant because the English Calais – the Calais Pale – was much larger than the present town, and reached out to the little towns or large villages of Ardres and Guines. Between these two places the English King Henry VIII and the French François I met at a famous conference in 1520, known to history as 'The Field of the Cloth of Gold'.

Just to the north of Calais lies the plain of Flanders, south of the Belgium frontier. The towns there and further east in Artois drew much of their wealth from the medieval cloth trade, which depended in turn on regular supplies of fine English wool from the Cotswolds, Yorkshire and East Anglia. The main towns wove their names into the history of the trade, so that Shakespeare's Polonius was 'stabb'd behind the Arras', a tapestry screen from that fine town of Picardy, and every lord and lady's cuff was once fringed with lace or linen from Cambrai – cambric. This trade reached its peak during the Hundred Years War, 1337–1453, when much of this part of France, outside the Calais Pale, was ruled by the Valois Dukes of Burgundy, who ruled Flanders and Artois from their northern capital in Brussels and were allies of Henry V and Henry VI, at least until 1435.

The Flanders plain, north of Calais and inland from Dunkirk, is flat and featureless, seamed by canals, with only the hill of Cassel standing out above the flood plain. Further inland, near Arras, the country rolls and ripples, so that Vimy Ridge, north of the town, now crowned by the Canadian War Memorial, was a strategic feature dominating the surrounding plains, and much fought over in the Great War. It affords fine views across to the brickworks and coalfields of Lens and the battlefields of Loos and Aubers Ridge, all marking terrible tragedies of war. I once cycled down The Old Front Line, from Ypres in Belgium to the banks of the River Somme, through a countryside littered with cemeteries. There are 218 British cemeteries in the Somme *département* alone, and a tour of the Great

War battlefields is just one way of exploring this part of France, where soldiers have been dying these thousand years or more.

To return to medieval times, the site of the 1346 Battle of Crécy can be found near Crécy-en-Ponthieu, just north of the River Somme, and the site of the Battle of Agincourt in 1415 also lies in this part of Picardy. The village is now called Azincourt and is on the Calais road, 10 miles north-east of Hesdin. Both places contain memorials to the battle and signboards describing the events which took place there. The 200-mile route of Henry V's army, from Harfleur near Le Havre to Calais, via Abbeville, Péronne and Albert, to Blagny and Agincourt, can be traced quite easily and is another theme for a car holiday. Moving on to other battlefields of the 1914–18 war, the Somme battlefield lies astride the old Roman road between the town of Albert, east of Amiens, and the small town of Baupaume. Here you will find those woods and villages with names long familiar from village-church memorials and regimental battle flags: Fricourt, Mametz, Delville Wood, High Wood, La Boiselle, and many more. If you look closely, the signs of battle are not hard to find – a trench line on the hill, the great mine crater by La Boiselle, and, everywhere, cemeteries.

For all its former sadness, this country of northern France is a very green and pleasant land, with an agreeable coastline on the Channel, and a hinterland full of small towns. A few places are well worth a longer stop: Amiens, Abbeville, Boulogne, St Valéry-sur-Somme, Arras, Le Touquet. My advice to anyone contemplating a visit to France is that this region deserves serious consideration, especially if you enjoy history, particularly military history, and take the time to look around. It is ideal country for the cycle-tourist and, being so close to England, is excellent for short, cross-Channel breaks by car. Boulogne is well worth a weekend visit, for it is a fine town with good shopping and restaurants, as well as being the centrepiece of the Côte d'Opale, which lies between Calais and the mouth of the Somme. Just past Cap Griz-Nez lies the little resort of Wissant, as well as the pin-bright little town of Montreuil-sur-Mer, which actually lies 3 miles inland. The more I think of this area, the more I recall what a pleasant place it is. I urge you to go there and see it for yourself.

Essential sights

The battlefields of Crécy and Agincourt. The town of Arras, particularly the Grande Place. Boulogne for shopping. The battlefields of the Somme, east of Albert. The Côte d'Opale, from Cap Gris-Nez south to the Somme estuary. Amiens for its cathedral and the water-gardens, the *hortillages*.

Food

The main dish I recall from this part of France is the *ficelle picarde*, a cheese and ham pancake formed into a roll, which I usually chose for my first course whenever I found it on a menu thereabouts. The local cuisine has been strongly influenced by that of Flanders, which is no bad thing as you can eat very well indeed in Flanders and Belgium. But it is hard to think of many dishes which are purely local, but *coqhuse* – pork and onions – is usually very good, as is *flamiche au poireaux*, leek tart. The seafood in Boulogne is usually excellent, hardly surprising, since this is France's main fishing port.

Cambrai produced nice, sticky mint-cakes with a curious name, *les bitesses de Cambrai*, which go well with coffee. From across the Belgium border, many restaurants offer *waterzooi*, which is a fish (or chicken) and vegetable stew in a cream sauce – well worth trying. Other dishes with a local tinge include *veau flamande* and *boeuf carbonnade* – beef in beer. In the slow rivers and canals, pike are common, so *quenelles de brochet* are usually worth trying, as are other rib-sticking dishes, such as the sausages, *andouillettes*, from Arras and Cambrai. To this list one can add local pâtés. Anything prepared *à la flamande* is made with onions or leeks or sometimes red cabbage. This is a working area and workers often have a sweet tooth, so the pastries and puddings are usually excellent. Others, like me, who prefer savoury dishes will find a good choice of cheeses, notably *Mont des Cats* from Flanders, *fromage fort de Béthune*, *boulette d'Avesnes* and *Maroilles*, a strong-flavoured cheese with a thick orange rind.

Wine

The big drink of northern France is beer. The wise visitor will ask for a *demi-pression* from the keg under the counter, for otherwise he or she will be given an expensive imported bottle – perhaps twice the price for half the quantity. Beer finds its way into the cooking, as in *boeuf carbonnade*. There is no local wine but those of nearby Champagne frequently filter across the frontier and most good restaurants will offer an adequate range of French wines.

RESTAURANTS

80100 Abbeville

HOTEL DE FRANCE
19 Place du Pilon
☎ (22) 24 00 42
This fairly large hotel (77 rooms) lies in the town centre. GB-plated cars get robbed with distressing frequency in northern France, so unload the car completely if you intend to stay overnight. This hotel-restaurant offers a good range of menus from F75 to F200. Good seafood and *ficelle picarde*, pancake with ham, mushrooms, fresh cream, grated cheese and cooked in the oven.

80300 Albert

HOTEL DE LA BASILIQUE
3 et 5 Rue Gambetta
☎ (22) 75 04 71
La Basilique accurately describes itself as a 'typical small town French hotel'. Albert is the centre for touring the battlefields of the Somme, which lie a mile or two outside the town, towards Baupaume. The F75 menu offers *ficelle picarde*, roast trout with sorrel, and homemade pastry.

62610 Ardres

HOTEL CLEMENT
Esplanade Maréchal Leclerc
☎ (21) 82 25 25
Just ten miles inland from Calais, the Hôtel Clément has long been popular with the British, and after a decline some years ago is now back on form and likely to remain so. The hotel (17 rooms) is beautiful, the rooms comfortable, the food good, though not particularly cheap, with menus ranging from F100 to F300. Excellent wines. Best to book. Restaurant closed Monday evening and Tuesday lunchtime.

62000 Arras

LE CHANZY
8 Rue Chanzy
☎ (21) 71 02 02
The Chanzy is a very typical French restaurant where the food matters more than the décor. The menus range from F100 to F180. Ask to see the wine cellars underneath the restaurant, for they

stretch for miles, hewed out of the chalk, and are an experience not every restaurant can offer. Rooms are also available at the Chanzy, so try here if the Grand Place hotels are full.

62200 Boulogne-Sur-Mer

L'HUITERIE
11 Place Lorraine
☎ (21) 31 35 27
The front of this excellent little restaurant is a fish shop, but don't be put off. Boulogne is the first fishing port of France but nowhere in town is the seafood better than here. Try the *assiette des fruits de mer* – vast – on the F180 menu.

LA MATELOTE
80 Boulevard Ste-Beuve
☎ (21) 30 17 97
The Matelote, opposite the Casino, has long been a favourite restaurant with British visitors, which may have contributed to a slowing down in the service and a hike in the prices. Even so, good food and a beautiful restaurant, plus a Michelin rosette. Menus from F150 to F300. Closed Sunday evening.

62100 Calais

LE CHANNEL
3 Boulevard de la Résistance
☎ (21) 34 42 30
This restaurant was recommended by two local people I accosted in the street, and the food bore out their recommendations. Menus from F70 to F250. Closed Sunday evening and Monday.

LA DILIGENCE
Rue Edmond Roche
☎ (21) 96 92 89
Calais has the reputation of being a gastronomic desert but you can eat well at this restaurant just off the Rue Royale, close to the popular Hôtel Meurice. Menus from F75 to F180.

RESTAURANT LA DUCHESSE
44 Rue du Duc de Guise
☎ (21) 97 59 69
A restaurant recommended by a knowledgeable friend, and good for *langoustines*, *sole meunière* and other fish dishes, but also for its excellent *filet de boeuf*. Menus from F98 to F250.

59400 Cambrai

AUBERGE LA CHOPE
17 Rue des Docks
☎ (27) 81 36 78
M. Roussel's small (12 rooms) hotel is an Auberge de la France, and offers good value for money, with rooms from F95 and menus from F58 to F100. Restaurant closed on Sunday.

62142 Colembert

HOSTELLERIE DU CHATEAU DES TOURELLES
On D127
Le Wast
☎ (21) 33 34 78
Inland from Boulogne, the hamlet of Le Wast is best known for this elegant hotel-restaurant, an excellent 2-star *logis* run by a young couple, the Feutrys. The dining room offers good food, sparkling glass, even a log fire in the winter. Well worth a visit. 16 rooms. Menus from F95 to F300. Restaurant closed Monday lunchtime. Best to book.

02380 Coucy-le-Château

HOTEL BELLE VUE
Porte de Laon
Ville Haute
☎ (23) 52 70 12
This little town in the Aisne was once crowned with the huge castle of the Lords of Coucy. You can read all about the Coucys in the Hundred Years War in Barbara Tuchman's *A Distant Mirror*. The Belle Vue has 10 inexpensive rooms and good menus from F80 to F170. Restaurant closed Tuesday and throughout February.

80150 Crécy-en-Ponthieu

HOTEL DE LA MAYE
13 Rue St Riquier
☎ (22) 23 54 35
Situated in the centre of this small town in the Somme, just below the 1346 battlefield where the Black Prince won his spurs, the Hôtel de la Maye is a plain but pleasant *logis* where M. Grévet serves remarkably good food. Try the salmon pancakes. Closed Monday.

80600 Doullens

HOTEL LE SULLY
45 Rue d'Arras
☎ (22) 77 10 87
This tiny, 2-star hotel, with just seven rooms, is a good centre for the Somme battlefields. Menus from F55 to F120. Closed Monday.

59240 Dunkirk

HOTEL DU XIXème SIECLE
1 Place de la Gare
☎ (28) 66 79 28
Dunkirk is not a pretty town but it has some remarkably good restaurants and one *logis* – this one – where M. Badts offers 14 rooms and good traditional menus from F65 to F105. Closed Sunday.

62270 Frévent

HOTEL D'AMIENS
7 Rue de Doullens
☎ (21) 03 65 43
M. Varga won the regional heat in the *Logis de France* Cookery Competition in 1987, and offers a high standard of cuisine and a warm welcome. Try his *pâté de truite des Trois Vallées du Ternoise*, an award-winning dish. The battlefield of Agincourt (Azincourt) is not far away and worth a visit. There are only 10 rooms, so it is best to book. Menus from F58 to F200.

HOTELLERIE LE VERT BOCAGE
Monchel-sur-Canche
☎ (21) 47 96 75
On arriving at this excellent, modern little hotel on a wild winter night we were met by the smell of good cooking and a huge log fire. Comfortable rooms and very good food, in a dining room looking out on a duck pond. Not easy to find – down the road to Flers, off the CD340 between Frévent and Hesdin – but worth the effort.

59190 Hazebrouck

AUBERGE DE LA FORET
La Motte au Bois
☎ (28) 48 08 78
M. Bécu's hotel is ideal for visiting the northern battlefields of the Great War, or for forays across the Belgian frontier to Ypres. 13 rooms. Menus from F110 to F220. Good wine list. Restaurant closed Sunday evening and Monday.

62140 Hesdin

HOTEL DES FLANDRES
22 Rue Arras
☎ (21) 86 80 21
This fine little 2-star *logis* gets into most of the guides because the food is first-class and good value, with menus from F57 to F180. A good place to stay when heading out or going home via Calais or Boulogne. There are only 14 rooms, so it is best to book.

62380 Lumbres

MOULIN DE MOMBRIEUX
Route de Bayenghem
☎ (21) 39 62 44
This excellent little hotel-restaurant, 7 miles west of St Omer on the road to Boulogne, has 4 stars and a Michelin rosette, as well as 20 rooms and a waterwheel. It is not cheap – menus and rooms both start at F175 – but M. Gaudry's food is worth every centime.

62170 Montreuil-sur-Mer

HOTEL BELLEVUE
6 Ave du 11 Novembre
☎ (21) 06 04 19
M. Héro's little hotel is a good place to stay while exploring this small town, now some way inland from the sea. 13 rooms and good menus from F60 to F150. The great local watering hole is the famous Château de Montreuil, which is now a splendid hotel. But you will also do very well at the Bellevue, from where you can explore the town centre on foot.

02170 Le Nouvion-en-Thiérache

HOTEL PETION
41 Rue Théodore-Blot
☎ (23) 97 00 11
The Thiérache, a region of villages, castles and fortified churches in northern France, was once the frontier between France and Flanders and is now part of the Aisne. It is off the too-well-travelled track and therefore well worth exploring. This 2-star little *logis*, with 12 rooms and menus from F45 to F190, would make a pleasant base for touring the Thiérache.

62500 St Omer

HOTEL LES FRANGINS
3 Rue Carnot
☎ (21) 38 12 47
We dined so well at Les Frangins that we almost missed the ferry. This 2-star *logis* has 20 rooms, with good menus from F57 to F155. The restaurant is closed for lunch on Friday. Try to fit this restaurant in when hurrying towards Calais or Boulogne.

80200 Péronne

HOSTELLERIE DES REMPARTS

☎ (22) 84 38 21
Péronne is an interesting fortified town on Henry V's route from Harfleur to Agincourt. M. Drichemont runs a very fine, rather old-fashioned hotel on traditional lines: comfortable beds, good food, and a smile. Menus from F65 to F200. Excellent wine list.

62360 Pont de Briques

HOTEL CLERY
Château Hesdin l'Abbé
Hesdin l'Abbé
☎ (21) 83 19 83
The elegant and beautiful Château Hesdin l'Abbé, just outside Boulogne, is a marvellous hotel. Only 5 miles from the ferry port, it is the perfect spot for a weekend break. Set in parkland, with beautiful rooms and marvellous food, it is a must for all true Francophiles. 18 rooms. Menus from F140 to F250. (Some people have also recommended the food at Le Manoir, on the main road at Pont de Briques.)

62520 Le Touquet

LE CAFE DES ARTS
80 Rue de Paris
☎ (21) 05 21 55
Le Touquet is such a pleasant, elegant resort that I am rather surprised more British people don't go there. It has plenty of good restaurants, but I chose this one for good food at moderate prices. Try the *saumon aux lentilles vertes*, and explore the cheese board. Menus from F120 to F220. Closed Monday and Tuesday.

62580 Vimy

HOTEL DU MANOIR
35 Route Nationale
Arras
☎ (21) 58 68 58
This 2-star *logis* is not actually in Arras but a little to the north at
Gavrelle, near Vimy Ridge, which is crowned by the great Canadian
War Memorial. A pleasant *logis* with good food at moderate prices.
Menus from F60 to F120. 20 rooms.

02600 Villers-Cotterêts

HOTEL DE L'ABBAYE
Rue des Tournelles
Longpont
☎ (23) 96 02 44
Most *logis* lie outside large towns as does this one at Longpont, south-
west of Soissons, in the Aisne. Yet it is close to the Ile de France, and
therefore a good touring base for the country north of Paris. 11 rooms.
Good menus from F80 to F200.

62126 Wimille

RELAIS DE LA BROCANTE
Near to the church
☎ (21) 83 19 31
This *relais*, three miles out of Boulogne on the Calais road, is now
said to offer the best value-for-money in or around Boulogne. In fact,
the *prix-fixe* menus are somewhat lean, but the *à la carte* is excellent
value. Try the *flamiche* of leeks and oysters, or any of the seafood
dishes.

59470 Wormhout

HOSTELLERIE ST LOUIS
47 Rue de L'Eglise
☎ (26) 68 81 83
This fine hotel in the Pas de Calais, set in the canal-seamed marches
of Flanders, is not the easiest place to find after dark, and you'll need
the Michelin map. The food is very good and the cellar remarkable. A
3-star *logis*, with 20 rooms. Menus from F100 to F250.

NORMANDY

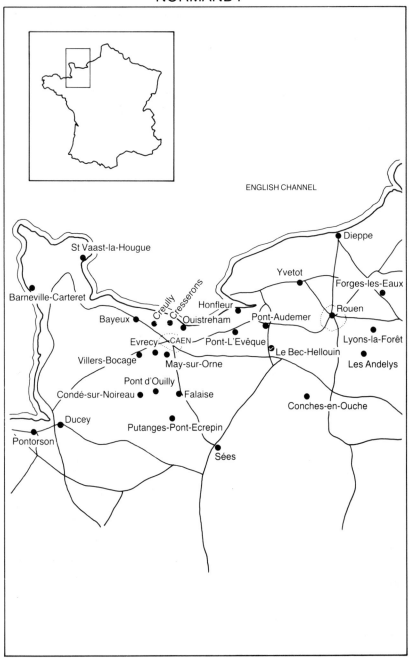

NORMANDY

Normandy, that ancient dukedom of the Plantagenet kings of England, has a lot to offer the gastronomically minded traveller. This is a province which possesses its own distinct regional cuisine, based on the fresh local produce provided by the dairy herds or the chill offshore waters. But while *haute cuisine* can be found in other parts of France, notably Burgundy and the Périgord, Normandy can also offer travellers from Britain proximity and ease of access. They can enter Normandy through four ports – Dieppe, Le Havre, Caen-Ouistreham and Cherbourg, and visitors from other European countries and North America will reach the province with ease via the Charles de Gaulle airport at Paris, and then down the excellent autoroutes into Normandy's fertile heartland.

Normandy has history as well as gastronomy to lure the traveller, and it makes sense for the visitor to combine the two. Few parts of France have so many fine towns, old castles, splendid scenery and good restaurants. The present province, which is largely the same in extent as the old Norman one, is divided into five *départements*: Seine-Maritime, Eure, Calvados, Orne in the south, and away to the west, Manche. This last *département* is largely occupied by the beautiful Cotentin peninsula, but the attractions of the province are best considered by touring from the north, and the wise first-time visitor to Normandy will begin the tour in the fine old seaport of Dieppe.

Unlike many Norman towns, Dieppe did not suffer too badly in the Second World War, although it was the setting for a tragic commando raid in 1942, when many brave Canadian soldiers were killed on the stony, shelving beach below the present promenade. The Canadian

War Cemetery lies on the headland to the south of the town. Dieppe is still a ferry port and resort town. Once very popular with the English, it attracted a large number of artists with its clear Channel light, and was a refuge for those people who, like Oscar Wilde, had blotted their copybooks at home. It remains a pleasant breezy place, with good shopping, adequate hotels, at least two good restaurants, and excellent access to the countryside beyond.

From Dieppe, one short excursion lies just inland, to see the great castle at Arques-la-Bataille, which has a good *logis* hotel, Au Vert Galant, just below the ramparts. Then let us head south, along the Channel coast, through a string of little seaside resorts and ports, Yport, Fécamp, St Valéry-en-Caux, which are little visited by foreigners and quite delightful. These resorts mark the edge of the *pays de Caux*, the chalk country of Normandy, which can be crossed in a south-easterly direction to the Valley of the Seine and Rouen. Places to visit in the hinterland of Seine-Maritime include the pretty town of Lyons-la-Forêt, which lies just in the Eure, and the spa at Forges-les-Eaux. The Seine is a very fine tidal river, and by sticking to the north bank as it winds inland, the traveller will pass Caudebec-en-Caux, another pleasant little town with several good hotels, before arriving at Rouen. The city's old town, around the Cathedral, is really the place to wander, but other sights include Rouen's medieval clock, the *Gros Horloge*, and the *Vieux Marché*, the Old Market where Joan of Arc was burned in 1431. Rouen is a very fine city, well worth a full day's visit. The river can be followed east from here, upstream towards the Vexin, the area bordering the Ile de France. On the way there the traveller should visit the castle of Richard Coeur de Lion at Les Andeleys – the Château-Gaillard or 'Saucy Castle' – the towns of Vernon and Mantes-la-Jolie, and Monet's house and gardens at Giverny.

The next *département*, which lies mostly on the south bank of the River Eure, is one of those parts of Normandy visitors often miss, a region of open fields and orchards; purely Norman, little touched by tourism. Places to visit here include Anet, which has a fine château, the town of Verneuil, the abbeys at Le Bec-Hellouin and Jumièges, and the valley of the River Risle, which leads up towards Pont-Audemer and the Calvados coast, where the essential stop on the western side of the bay of the Seine is the port and artists' centre of Honfleur. This looks out across the estuary to the oil refineries of Le Havre and all that is left of Shakespeare's 'girded Harfleur', both of which have more utility than beauty. But Honfleur is a gem, with several good hotels and restaurants. Allow a full day for this delightful port, before turning west to the smart towns of Trouville and Deauville, and so to the D-Day beaches.

Trouville, Deauville and Cabourg are Thirties-style resorts, matched inland by such towns as Lisieux, which is a pilgrimage centre and the home of Saint Thérèse, and the cheese centre of Pont-l'Evêque. Pressing on, the traveller soon comes to the D-Day beaches and the battlefields of 1944, which begin at Ranville and Merville, just east of the River Orne. The D-Day beaches continue west to the Cotentin, past a string of little ports and resorts, each with its memorials and museums – Luc-sur-Mer, Llon-sur-Mer, St Aubin and Arromanches, where there is a fine D-Day Museum. This area now forms part of the Commando Trail, which links to the Pegasus Trail, the route of the British 6th Airborne Division, at Pegasus Bridge, 6 miles up the Caen Canal from the port of Ouistreham. The boats of Brittany Ferries from Portsmouth now berth daily at Ouistreham. All these places have adequate-to-good restaurants and comfortable *logis* hotels, fronted by vast, sandy beaches, some still with their D-Day codenames – 'Gold', 'Juno', 'Sword', for the British and Canadian beaches, and for the Americans, 'Omaha'. The huge American Cemetery at St Laurent, behind 'Omaha', is a tragic yet beautiful place. Nor should you leave this coast without visiting the new *Musée de la Paix* at Caen, which tells the full story of the Normandy fighting.

An older, but still embattled Normandy lies behind the D-Day coast, notably in the towns of Caen and Bayeux, both of which must be visited on any tour of the province. Caen has William the Conqueror's old castle and two great Abbeys, the Abbaye aux Hommes, built by William, and the Abbaye aux Dames, built by his wife Mathilda, as a penance for their having married within the limits of consanguinity. It also has many good hotels and restaurants, and some fine shopping streets and public buildings, most of the latter in fine, white Caen stone.

Much of old Caen was destroyed in the fighting of June and July 1944, but Bayeux, a little further west, was captured quickly on the evening of D-Day and so escaped a similar fate. Bayeux therefore feels like a much older town than Caen and remains a place of narrow, cobbled streets and quiet squares, its main attraction being the famous Bayeux tapestry (actually a Saxon embroidery), quite beautiful and well worth seeing.

We are now well into the Calvados *département*, a fairly well-visited part of Normandy, so to get off the beaten track we must go either south or west, into the Manche or the Orne. South of Caen, through Maye-sur-Orne and Thury-Harcourt, lies the hilly country of the Suisse Normande, a place of small towns and villages, rather like the English Peak District, perfect for walking. The best way into and through the Suisse Normande is along the valley of the Orne, through Clécy, Pont d'Ouilly, and Putanges-Pont d'Ecrepin from where the wise visitor will divert east, still in the Calvados, for a visit to Falaise, birthplace of William the Conqueror, which has a fine castle and a very beautiful church. South of Putanges the visitor enters the Orne *département*, the forested frontier, where the little spa of Bagnoles de l'Orne and the town of Carrouges are worth a visit, before the southern limit of Normandy is finally reached at the town of Alençon. Alençon is famous for lace, the *point d'Alençon*, and is surrounded by attractive, rolling countryside.

Finally – although one could list the attractions of Normandy almost endlessly – there comes the western *département* of the Manche. There, on the northern tip of the Cotentin peninsula, lies Cherbourg as the access port. Cherbourg is not attractive, but to the east lies the Val du Saire, and little ports such as Barfleur and St Vaast-la-Hogue. South of St Vaast lies the other American invasion beach, 'Utah', and just inland from there lies the little village of Ste-Mère-Eglise, liberated by American paratroops on the night of 5–6 June 1944, and now containing the interesting Airborne Museum, set under a parachute-style roof. There is also a beautiful stained-glass memorial window in the church, and a famous horse-market.

Those who prefer to avoid the more popular routes could drive down the west coast of the Cotentin, from Goury on the Nez de Jobourg to Barneville-Carteret, a little port, and Portbail, set among the sand dunes, on to places such as Coutances, which has a fine cathedral, then on to Granville and St Jean-le-Thomas. South from here lie the fine towns of Avranches and, a little west, St Hilaire-du-Harcourt, Mortain and beautiful Domfront.

Normandy is a fine, lush, green, agricultural province, full of beautiful places to see, with many interesting museums and historic sites. The wise visitor will select a few of the principal attractions according to taste and spend the rest of the time just exploring.

Essential sights

The Bayeux Tapestry in Bayeux, the D-Day Museum at Arromanches, and the new *Musée de la Paix* in Caen. The cities of Caen, Bayeux and Rouen – allow a full day for each. The abbeys at Le Bec-Hellouin and Jumièges on the Seine. The American Cemetery at St Laurent above 'Omaha' Beach is very impressive. To go off the beaten track, visit the Suisse Normande, south of Caen, or the western coast of the Contentin peninsula. The road up the Seine Valley from Honfleur to Les Andelys is a delightful journey.

Food

The Normans are farmers and fishing folk, with little time for the nuances of life. This fact is reflected in the cooking, which tends to produce dishes swathed in rich sauces made with the principal local products, butter, cream, Calvados (cider brandy) or cider. The most famous regional dish is probably *tripes à la mode de Caen*, which I have never forced myself to try, but I watch with horrified fascination when my colleagues down it with gusto. Norman pork sausages – *andouilles* or *andouillettes*, are rather more to my taste. Other dishes I can recommend are the *veau* or *poulet Vallée d'Auge*, which comes with a triple sauce of cream, cider and Calvados, *moules à la Normande*, best found in Port-en-Bessin or Courseulles, the *ficelle Normande*, not unlike that ham-and-cheese rolled pancake found in Picardy, or the local fish and shellfish. Dieppe has several excellent seafood restaurants, and in a maritime province such as Normandy, the lobsters and fish are especially excellent. Try the *sole Normande*, in which the fish comes in a cream sauce with cider, or the *demoiselles à la crème* (small lobsters in a cream sauce), or the Rouen duck, or *moules à la crème*, or lamb from the Cotentin.

It should be clear by now that any dish *à la Normande* comes with a cream and Calvados sauce, which leads on to the other features of the Norman landscape – dairy cows and apple orchards. These cows produce the cream and the wherewithal for that vast range of Normandy cheeses, of which the best known is Camembert. This cheese was invented in 1790 by a Norman dairymaid, Marie Harel, and there is a statue to her memory in the village of Camembert. The others are Liverot, Pont-L'Evêque and Neufchâtel, but any decent cheeseboard will offer other Norman cheeses as well – Bondard, Carré de Bray, Briquebec from the Cotentin – while for pudding I suggest *teurgoule*, rather like rice pudding, and a speciality of the Vallée d'Orne.

Wine

Normandy does not have a local wine of its own, but most of the seafood and many of the chicken and veal dishes go very well with a chilled Muscadet from the Loire region to the south. However, the great drink of Normandy is cider, produced from those small, red cider apples which turn the summer orchards into bright patches of colour. The usual mealtime drink is *cidre-bouché*, the sparkling version that comes either dry (*sec* or *brut*) or sweet (*doux*). Do not be misled into thinking this beverage is innocuous. A bottle or two can buckle the strongest knees.

Calvados is brandy distilled from cider and it is the custom to take *un Calva*, a shot of Calvados in the middle of the meal, in order to create space for yet more food. This drink, downed in one, is called *le trou Normand* – the Norman hole – and some restaurants offer it without being asked. The excellent Calvados is also drunk before and after meals, and the finest distillations come from the Vallée d'Auge. The other local drink, a world-famous *digestif*, is Bénédictine, which was invented by a monk at the Abbey of Fécamp, and is still manufactured within the town.

RESTAURANTS

27700 Les Andelys

LA CHAINE D'OR
27 Rue Grande
☎ (32) 54 00 31
For many the attraction at Les Andelys is the Château-Gaillard, but take time to dine or lunch at this pleasant hotel beside the Seine. Try the trout. Restaurant closed Sunday evening and Monday. Menus from F120 to F260. The hotel is very popular at weekends, so it is best to book.

50270 Barneville-Carteret

HOTEL LES ISLES
Barneville plage
☎ (33) 04 90 76
The western coast of the Contentin is worth visiting, for it lies off the beaten track. This fine hotel lies above a good beach, with sweeping views out to the Channel Islands. Excellent shellfish and seafood. 30 rooms. Menus from F70 to F220.

14400 Bayeux

HOTEL DU LION D'OR
71 Rue St Jean
☎ (31) 92 06 90
The Lion d'Or has a Michelin rosette, is one of the few 3-star *logis*, and is a very fine hotel with a first-class restaurant. Menus from F100 to F240. Try the *omelette de homard* or any of the dishes recommended by the chef. 28 rooms and very good service.

HOTEL DU LUXEMBOURG
25 Rue des Bouchers
☎ (31) 92 00 04
The Luxembourg is said to be the best hotel in Bayeux, and has food to match, demonstrating this fact by coming second in the Brittany Ferries Restaurant Competition with its F99 menu. The service is first-class, the hotel quite small, with only 19 rooms. Well worth a visit, but it is best to book.

27800 Le Bec-Hellouin

AUBERGE DE L'ABBAYE
Town centre
☎ (32) 44 86 02
I thought I saw a ghost outside this hotel one night, but it turned out to be a monk from the abbey. Mme Sergent has maintained a very high level of Norman cuisine, served in a dining room which sparkles with glass and polished brass. Try the apple and Calvados pie. Menus from F120 to F250. 8 rooms. Restaurant closed Monday evening and Tuesday outside the summer months.

27190 Conches-en-Ouche

HOTEL LE CYGNE
36 Rue du Val
☎ (32) 30 20 60
The Cygne is a 1-star *logis*, set in an old post-house. The food is rustic Norman, rich and filling. Menus from F70 to F100. 15 rooms. Restaurant closed Monday.

14110 Condé-sur-Noireau

AUBERGE ST GERMAIN
St Germain du Crioult
☎ (31) 69 08 10
This little hotel is run on traditional lines, M. Baude doing the cooking and Mme Baude running the dining room. St Germain is 2 miles from Condé, at the entrance to the Suisse Normande, and the hotel offers menus from F55 to F97, excellent value for money, including regional dishes such as *château flambé au Calvados* and *sorbet à la pomme au Calvados*.

114440 Cresserons

LA VALISE GOURMANDE
7 Route de Lion sur Mer
☎ (16) 31 37 39 10
A restaurant offering excellent value in a very pretty village between Caen and Luc, and which featured well in the Brittany Ferries Restaurant Competition. For F200 you will dine like a king. If the weather is fine, lunch on the terrace.

14480 Creully

HOSTELLERIE ST-MARTIN
6 Place Edmond Paillaud
☎ (31) 80 10 11
This pleasant 2-star *logis*, just off the D-Day beaches, 5 miles southwest of Courseulles, serves Normandy specialities and excellent seafood. 8 rooms. Menus from F49 to F110. Restaurant closed Sunday evening and Monday.

76200 Dieppe

LE RELAIS GAMBETTA
95 Avenue Gambetta
☎ (35) 84 12 91
Dieppe has many hotels and several good restaurants, but only one *logis*. This is quite small (18 rooms) but has a good restaurant serving local specialities and menus from F75 to F160. Restaurant closed Sunday evening and Monday.

150220 Ducey

AUBERGE DE LA SELUNE
Village centre
☎ (33) 48 53 62
M. Girres won the Basse-Normandie heat of the *Logis de France* Cookery Contest with his *pie au crabe*. A nice hotel (20 rooms) with an excellent F85 menu. Menus range from F48 to F145. Restaurant closed Monday. Highly recommended.

14210 Evrecy

AUBERGE DU PONT DE BRIE
Goupillières
☎ (31) 79 37 84
This elegant 10-bedroom *logis* tucked away at Goupillières, in the green valley of the Orne, south of Caen, made me very welcome on

the second day of my walk across France. I left my muddy boots at the door. Mme Dri runs a tight ship, offering good service and first-class food in a splendid dining room. The hotel is almost perfect, and since it is not far from Caen it is ideal for a weekend break. Menus from F70 to F220. Restaurant closed Wednesday.

14700 Falaise

HOTEL DE LA POSTE
38 Rue Georges Clemenceau
☎ (31) 90 13 14
Falaise, the birthplace of William the Conqueror, is a very fine town and has an equally fine castle. The Hôtel de la Poste is a good *logis*, with a restaurant serving Norman country cooking and seafood. 18 rooms and menus from F85 to F155. Restaurant closed Sunday evening and Monday.

76440 Forges-les-Eaux

HOTEL DE LA PAIX
17 Rue de Neufchatel
☎ (35) 90 51 22
M. Michel of the Hôtel de la Paix has a fine and well-deserved reputation for the excellence of his food, and his wine list is almost as remarkable. The small hotel (only five rooms) is an old timbered building with a delightful dining room. Menus from F60 to F130. Restaurant closed Sunday evening and Monday.

St Germain de Tallevende

AUBERGE DE ST GERMAIN
Place de l'Eglise
☎ (31) 68 24 13
This *logis* near Vire, in the Bocage, won the Brittany Ferries Restaurant Competition for Normandy in 1988. A pleasant little place, with only three rooms but a good F85 menu. Worth the detour. Restaurant closed Monday.

114600 Honfleur

HOSTELLERIE LECHAT
Place Ste Cathérine
☎ (31) 89 23 85
The situation alone almost makes a meal at the Hostellerie Léchat worth while, in this pretty little port by the Seine estuary. Try the seafood platter.

27480 Lyons-la-Forêt

HOTEL LA LICORNE
Town centre
☎ (32) 49 62 02
Lyons-la-Forêt is a pleasant little half-timbered town, deep in the woods, and the Licorne is a well-patronized hotel, one of several in the town centre. The dining room is small, so it is best to reserve a table. Menus from F135 to F210. 21 rooms. Restaurant closed Sunday evening.

14320 May-sur-Orne

HOTEL L'AMMONITE
Route de Caen
☎ (31) 79 80 27
L'Ammonite, a few miles south of Caen, is not an establishment for the glitterati, but Mme Horel and her husband Jean-Claude will make you feel very welcome. Inexpensive menus from F45 to F85.

14150 Ouistreham

HOTEL LA NORMANDIE
71 Avenue Michel Cabieu
☎ (31) 97 17 57
A very pleasant and rather smart *logis*, close to the port and so ideal for a last lunch before the 4 o'clock ferry. Try the *côte de veau* with Camembert sauce. Menus from F95 to F230. 13 rooms. Closed Sunday evening and Monday. This seaport is at the heart of the D-Day Coast and is famous for freshly landed seafood.

27500 Pont-Audemer

LES CLOCHES DE CORNEVILLE
Route de Rouen
Corneville-sur-Risle
☎ (32) 57 01 04
This pebble-dashed *logis* set on a small hill, has red umbrellas in the garden and very good food in a dining room which looks out across the Risle valley, west of the seine. Norman dishes. 12 rooms. Well worth a visit. Menus from F125. Restaurant closed Wednesday.

14130 Pont-L'Evêque

AUBERGE LA HAUQUERIE
On Rn 175 at Quettéville
☎ (31) 64 14 46
This *logis* is in the countryside, six miles from Pont-l'Evêque on the N175 towards Quetteville. It was once a farm and is now a small hotel with just eight rooms. The dining room looks out over lawns to Mme Lombard's stud farm. A good centre for visiting the Normandy coast. Menus from F80 to F210.

14690 Pont d'Ouilly

AUBERGE ST CHRISTOPHE
Town centre
☎ (31) 69 81 23
The St Christophe, a little south of Caen, is one of those delightful country hotels seemingly held together by ivy. The dining room is elegant, the seven bedrooms rather small, the F70 menu excellent value. Well worth a stop. Restaurant closed Sunday evening and Monday.

50170 Pontorson

HOTEL MONTGOMERY
13 Rue Couesnon
☎ (33) 60 00 09
Mme Le Bellegard's Hôtel Montgomery recalls the famous Montgomerys of the past, including the General of 8th Army and D-Day fame. The hotel was once the *logis* of the Counts of Montgomery and is full of antique furniture, as well as being a gastronomic centre close to Mont-St-Michel. 32 rooms and menus from F68 to F140. Restaurant closed Tuesday evening and Wednesday.

61210 Putanges-Pont-Ecrepin

HOTEL DU LION VERD
Town centre
☎ (33) 35 01 86
This hotel lies at the foot of the town, close to the Orne. It is a 2-star establishment, well run, not over-friendly, but with excellent food, and is a good stopping point halfway from the Channel to the Loire. 20 rooms and menus from F50 to F180.

76000 Rouen

LA CACHE-RIBAUD
10 Rue de Tambour
☎ (35) 71 04 82
A small, attractive restaurant, tucked away just off the Rue Jeanne
d'Arc, serving Norman specialities. Excellent for lunch with a good
F60 menu and a vast *carte*.

61500 Sées

HOTEL LE CHEVAL BLANC
1 Place St Pierre
☎ (33) 27 80 48
Sées is a pleasant town with a huge market hall, a fine cathedral and
Le Cheval Blanc. Good food and helpful staff. Menus from F56 to
F180, and a very good wine list. Restaurant closed Thursday evening
and Friday.

LE DAUPHIN
31 Place des Halles
☎ (33) 27 80 07
This restaurant is highly recommended, both for the variety of the
F100 menu and the excellent food. Try the trout with apple, the
poached eggs with *crevettes*. Don't miss this restaurant if you are near
Sées. Other menus from F85 to F220. Restaurant closed Monday.

HOTEL L'ILE DE SEES
Macé
Near Sées
☎ (33) 27 98 65
Macé is a suburb of Sées, most notable for the 2-star *logis*, L'Hôtel de
l'Ile. There are 16 rooms, a cheerful dining room, good food and a
warm welcome from M. Orcier. Well worth dining here, with menus
from F78 to F150. Restaurant closed Sunday evening and Monday.

50550 St Vaast-la-Hougue

HOTEL DE FRANCE ET FUCHSIAS
18 Rue Maréchal Foch
☎ (33) 54 42 26
Set to the east of Cherbourg, on the top of the Cotentin, this well-
known and popular hotel has maintained high standards in the face
of popularity. This is a favourite spot for visiting yachtsmen and
people using the ferry port at Cherbourg. The restaurant serves
excellent seafood. 32 rooms. Menus from F60 to F200. Booking
advised. Restaurant closed Monday.

14310 Villers-Bocage

LES TROIS ROIS
Route de Vire
☎ (31) 77 00 32
A fine little *logis* restaurant with 14 rooms at the foot of the Cotentin.
Menus from F120 to F200, and excellent value. Try the fresh salmon
or the tuna. Restaurant closed Sunday evening and Monday.

76190 Yvetot

AUBERGE DU VAL-AU-CESNE
Le Val-au-Cesne
☎ (35) 56 63 06
This *auberge* is not easy to find, off the D5 between Yvetot and
Fréville, but the food is excellent and the accommodation comfortable. Our bill for two for an excellent dinner came to F180. Five
rooms.

BRITTANY

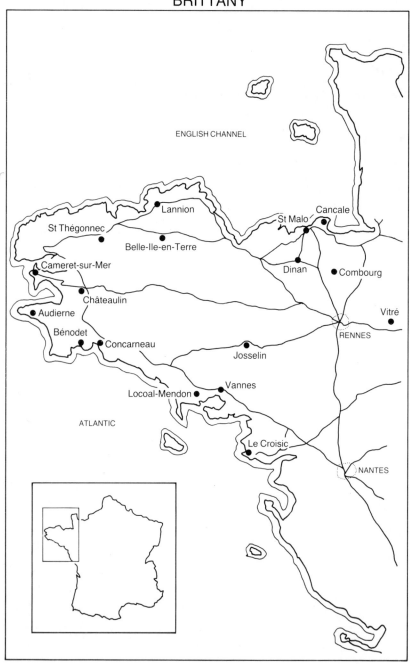

ENGLISH CHANNEL

Lannion

St Thégonnec

Belle-Ile-en-Terre

Cameret-sur-Mer

Châteaulin

Audierne

Bénodet

Concarneau

St Malo

Cancale

Dinan

Combourg

Vitré

RENNES

Josselin

Locoal-Mendon

Vannes

ATLANTIC

Le Croisic

NANTES

BRITTANY

Brittany is one of my favourite parts of France, and since it enjoys a considerable influx of British and other visitors every summer I think I can safely assume that my liking for it is shared by many of those not lucky enough to live within its boundaries. This is a little difficult to explain in a book designed for Francophiles, because Brittany is not a 'typical' province of France. Indeed there are those who claim that Brittany is not really French at all, and there are good reasons for this belief.

To begin with, the indigenous population, the Bretons, are Celts, not Gauls or Franks. They have close links with the Welsh, the Cornish, the Galicians of north-west Spain, people and countries which Brittany and the Bretons closely resemble. The differences from the rest of France can be noticed immediately on entering Brittany, but will be even more apparent as the traveller heads south or west into the *départements* of Morbihan or Finistère, where the Breton language can still be heard, where more people wear traditional dress, and the old ways still cling on. Modern Brittany now occupies much of the historic province that was once called Armorica, the 'Land facing the Sea', and although the ancient capital of Nantes has been hived off and attached to the region of Loire-Atlantique, I include it here, in Brittany, where it properly belongs.

The modern province of Brittany consists of four large *départements* – Ille-et-Vilaine, which contains Rennes, the present capital of Brittany; Côtes-du-Nord; Finistère; and down in the south, Morbihan. Each of these *départements* has something special to offer and each is different from all the others. The only real problem with a visit to Brittany is where to go, but at least the start is easy, for there are three obvious access ports – Cherbourg in the north of the Norman Cotentin, which puts the Côtes-du-Nord and Ille-et-Vilaine in easy reach, and the two Brittany Ferries ports actually within the province, the corsair city of St Malo in the Côtes-du-Nord, and Roscoff, far to the west in Finistère. Therefore, to keep it logical, let us begin in the east on the Breton-Norman border, at Mont-St-Michel, which now lies, just, in Normandy. This is due to the action of the River Cousenon – pronounced *kway-non* – the historic river boundary which once flowed round the eastern walls of Mont-St-Michel, but which, by switching to the west side during a storm some centuries ago, transferred the glories of Mont-St-Michel from Brittany to Normandy.

Fortunately you need not go far to find considerable compensations. For the first, go west to the famous oyster port of Cancale and dine on shellfish and seafood anywhere along the quays. Then move on to St Malo, a walled town full of hotels and restaurants set inside the ancient, if restored, walls – the *intra muros* – wandering up and down narrow, cobbled streets. A walk around the ramparts is the perfect way to walk off a lunch or dinner and takes the visitor past the island of the *Grande Bé*, where the writer Chateaubriand lies buried. South of St Malo lies the resort of Dinard, while up the River Rance lies the medieval town of Dinan, home of the famous Breton knight Bertrand du Guesclin, who became Constable of France in the fourteenth century and drove the English from most of their French possessions. There is a fine equestrian statue of Bertrand in full armour in the square in Dinan, and his heart lies in the town church.

South of Dinan lies Rennes, which has some excellent public buildings and is a fine city. But to complete a little tour of eastern Brittany, go east from Rennes to Vitré and Fougères, two towns on the frontier with the rest of France. Both have well preserved medieval castles and are definitely not to be missed, before returning to the coast via Dol-de-Bretagne, for a tour westwards along the coast of Côtes-du-Nord.

This northern coast is a beautiful mix of rocky headlands and long, sandy beaches studded with villages and attractive towns, so the visitor can wander at will. I can personally recommend Dinard, an Edwardian resort across the harbour from St Malo, Les Sables d'Or, which has a magnificent beach, Paimpol, Tréguier, Perros-Guirec, Trégastel, and the entire *Granit Rose* coast north-west of St Brieuc, so called because of its pink rock. The hinterland of this coast is green and rolling, with a number of small greystone villages set among folded hills, not dramatic perhaps but still very attractive. Go south into the centre of the province and visit Josselin, to see the great

Mont St Michel, Normandy

Port Racine, the smallest harbour in France, on the tip of the Cotentin peninsula near Cherbourg

Ste Mère-Église on the Cotentin peninsula

The port of Barfleur, near Cherbourg

Telgruc-sur-Mer, Brittany (photo: Paddy Hicks)

The clock tower in Dinan,
Brittany

Pointe du Raz, Brittany

castle of the Dukes of Rohan, or little towns like Pontivy, before heading west again into the most curious and Breton part of Brittany, Finistère.

Finistère, the 'end of the earth', is a jagged, wolf's head of a peninsula that juts out into the wild Atlantic, with the Ile d'Ouessant (Ushant) and the rock-littered seascapes of the Raz du Sein providing small barriers to the western ocean. This is a sea-girt coast, wildly attractive, with a great many places worth visiting. List Le Folgoët, Le Conquet, Plougastel, Camaret, Morgat, Locronon, Douarnenez, Audierne, Pont-l'Abbé and Bénodet as pegs to hang the journey on as you travel in and around these rocky headlands from north to south. Of all these, Douarnenez and Locronon are two beatiful places I would definitely not miss, and of the three western peninsulas, the central one of Crozon is my personal favourite.

The great feature of Brittany is the *parish-clos*, known in English as a parish close, a church and churchyard set off by a huge cross, or calvary, elaborately carved with stories from the Bible and quite remarkable. They are also quite rare, or at least by no means as common as their use on Breton tourist posters might lead you to expect. The best calvaries and *parish-clos* lie in the north of Finistère, south of Roscoff, in three villages, Ste Thégonnec, Guimiliau and Lampaul-Guimiliau, so one or all of these have to be seen. They are all quite close together. The countryside of Finistère is more dramatic than that of Ille-et-Vilaine, and possesses several groups of hills – the Monts d'Arrée and the tallest hill hereabouts, the Ménez-Hom near Châteaulin, from the top of which there are marvellous views over the western seascapes. Here too lies the *Argoat*, the 'country of wood'; the hinterland of Brittany around Huelgoat, although most of the old Celtic forests have been felled.

To continue the journey along the south coast is not a bad idea, because attractive and varied places will continue to appear, and the summer weather is usually both warmer and drier. Inland from Bénodet lies the cathedral city of Quimper and across the estuary lies another attractive fishing port, Concarneau, while to the east, at Pont-Aven, Gauguin had a studio. East again lies Lorient, once the home port for the French East India Company, the *Compagnie de L'Orient* (hence the name) a great German submarine base in the Second World War. Upstream from here lies Hennebont, which has medieval walls, but the finest walled city in the Morbihan is certainly Vannes, which lies on the north shore of the *Mor-bi-han* – the 'little sea', a vast estuary and salt-water lake formed by the arms of land reaching out into the sea at Quiberon and Port Navalo. The 'little sea' can be toured by the boats of the *Vedettes-Vertes* from Vannes, and those who came south to the Morbihan can also visit Belle-Ile from the port of Quiberon and see the famous menhirs or standing stones at Carnac, a sight to surpass Stonehenge.

Leave the beaten track to visit the peninsula east of the Morbihan and see St Gildas-de-Rhuys, where Abelard, the lover of Héloise, was once the abbot, and the castle at Sarzeau, where the repairs to the breach in the walls made by Du Guesclin can still be picked out among the stones. Move on to the port at Le Croisic, one of my favourite places in Brittany, and the great beach resort of La Baule, and then on to the shipbuilding centre at St Nazaire, at the mouth of the Loire, famous for the commando raid of 1942. Upstream from here lies Nantes, a very fine and large provincial city, with the great castle of the Dukes of Brittany and much to see and do.

Visitors to Brittany often explore the coast and neglect the hinterland. While this is quite understandable, the inland parts also have their attractions. I suggest a visit to the walking centre of Huelgoat, near the Monts d'Arrée or to the moorlands of the Landes de Lanvaux and the pretty town of Rochefort-en-Terre, west of Redon, north of the Morbihan. Those who like the countryside could follow the River Vilaine from Redon to Rennes and then go up the Rance and the Ille towards Dinan and St Malo. Brittany is a large province where visitors can tour year after year and never go the same way twice, ideal for walking, cycling or touring by car.

Essential sights

The calvaries and *parish-clos* of Finistère. St Malo, Dinan, Locronon, Rochefort-en-Terre, Douarnenez, Vitré, Fougères. For shopping, Nantes and Rennes are excellent. Open-air excursions are better in the south and west, to the Quiberon peninsula or across to Belle-Ile, or on the *Vedettes Vertes* boats around the Morbihan sea. Inland, cruising the Breton canals makes an excellent holiday, but Josselin, with its great castle, just has to be seen, even by car. Ask at the Tourist Offices to see if any *pardons* – local pilgrimages – are being held. See the menhirs and stone rows at Carnac in the Morbihan, and do not fail to visit Tréguier on the *Granit Rose* northern coast. In the north, Dinan, Dol and Cancale are all well worth a visit.

Food

I recall disembarking at St Malo with a friend of mine, all set for a *tour gastronomique* and as we rumbled up the link-span he remarked, 'The only thing I can't stand is seafood.' Since seafood is the main attraction of the Breton cuisine, I found this information dispiriting. But if you like oysters or mussels, crabs or lobster, sole or sea-bass, or any kind of sea or shellfish, this is the province for you. The seafood of Brittany, drawn from those chill Channel or Atlantic waters, is superb. Fortunately for my friend, so too is the poultry, the pork and the mutton. So whatever your preference, you will certainly not starve. There is also excellent lamb or mutton from the salt-flats and marshes near Mont-St-Michel, excellent chicken, especially the *poulet blanc Breton*, good sausages, *pâtés de campagne* and black or white pudding, *boudin*, and for smaller snacks the excellent *crêpes* and *galettes*.

These last two are the most typically Breton dish, little more than a large snack. They are rolled pancakes filled with anything from ice-cream to bacon and eggs, sweet fillings for the *crêpes*, savoury for the buckwheat *galettes*, and both are quite delicious. Every town and village, almost every street, will have its *crêperie* and a well-filled *galette* makes the perfect quick lunch, an ideal meal for the children. On the coast most of the restaurants will also offer *cotriade*, a fish stew, full of bits of this and that, but if you want a dish fit for a king, then the local speciality is *l'homard à l'Américaine*, which suffix is a corruption of the original *l'homard à l'Armorique*, which comes with garlic, cognac and a cream sauce. For other local dishes try the *gigot pré-salé*, the salt lamb from near Mont-St-Michel, any of the various oysters, or a huge dish of *moules* – mussels. Near Châteaulin look out for *saumon à la crème*, for this is a centre for salmon. Then there is mackerel from Quimper, though catches are in decline, and omelettes stuffed with tuna fish. The local Breton pudding is the *far Breton*, a custard tart including raisins, and rather sweet. Most of the cheeses come from nearby Normandy, although the *fromage Nantais* and Emmental are sometimes available. The vegetables, and in particular the asparagus and artichokes from Finistère, are always fresh and excellent.

Wine

The most common bottle seen on a Breton table is one containing cider, *cidre-bouché*, but close on its heels comes Muscadet, that young white wine from the region south of Nantes, which goes so well with the Breton seafood. There are three main types, of which the best is the Muscadet de Sèvre-et-Maine, the others being Muscadet and Muscadet des Côteaux de la Loire. The Gros-Plant Muscadet, if slightly rougher, is still excellent. Muscadet described as *sur lie* – on the lees – has been allowed to rest in the vat for a while before being bottled and is therefore rather more fruity than the others.

All decent Breton restaurants will offer a range of Muscadets and a good range of other French wines, red, white and rosé. Brittany favours oysters, the lobsters and fresh-caught fish, so Muscadet or *cidre-bouché* may be the best drink with most of the meals.

RESTAURANTS

29113 Audierne

HOTEL DE LA BAIE DES TREPASSES
Plogoff (Pointe du Raz)
☎ (98) 70 61 34
The Baie des Trépassés is on a wild part of the Brittany coast, but well seen from the dining room of this attractive hotel above the beach. A good four-course menu will cost no more than F75. Menus ranging from F70 to F220 offer a good range of Breton dishes and excellent local seafood. 27 rooms. Well worth a visit.

LE GOYEN
Sur Le Port
☎ (98) 70 08 88
A Michelin rosette is some indication of the quality of the food, wine and service in this fine hotel-restaurant by the harbour. Menus from F130 to F320. Try the seafood platters and the *parfait de pigeon au foie gras*. 29 rooms. Restaurant closed Monday.

22810 Belle-Ile-en-Terre

LE RELAIS DE L'ARGOAT
Rue de Guic
☎ (96) 43 00 34
This restaurant of the Côtes-du-Nord is very popular with the local people, which is always a good sign. Children welcome and good menus from F60 to F200. 18 rooms. Recommended. Restaurant closed Sunday evening and Monday.

29118 Bénodet

LA FERME DU LETTY
Letty (1½ miles from Bénodet)
☎ (98) 57 01 27
Another excellent restaurant, with one Michelin rosette gained by the cooking skills of young M. Guilbault, son of the proprietor. An immaculate little restaurant, not to be missed by lovers of good food. Menus from F200 to F400.

HOTEL DE LA POSTE
Rue de l'Eglise
☎ (98) 57 01 09
Bénodet has no less than four *logis* hotels and plenty of good restaurants, but this one is well sited and serves good local food. Menus from F60 to F200. 18 rooms. Restaurant closed Monday.

29129 Cameret-sur-Mer

HOTEL DE FRANCE
Sur le Port
☎ (98) 27 93 06
M. Moreau of this 2-star *logis* won the Brittany heat in the *Logis de France* Cookery Competition with his *homard (ou langouste) grillé à l'estragon frais*, so those who like a good lobster should stop here while touring Finistère. 22 rooms. Menus from F60 to F260. Restaurant closed Friday.

35260 Cancale

LE CANCALAISE
Quai Gambetta
☎ (99) 89 61 93
Cancale is full of good restaurants set around the harbour, but few are as good as this one. Try the local oysters with a bottle of chilled Muscadet. Menus from F135 to F230. 8 rooms.

HOTEL EMERAUDE
7 Quai Thomas
☎ (99) 89 61 76
The Emeraude has comfortable rooms and one of those dining rooms where you know you will dine well, perhaps on the terrace if the evening is warm. 16 rooms. Menus from F80 to F195. Restaurant closed Tuesday.

HOTEL DE LA POINTE DU GROUIN
On headland at Pointe de Grouin
☎ (99) 89 60 55
This hotel lies on the headland looking out onto the Baie de Mont-St-Michel. Very smart, with a dining room looking over the sea. Good menus, featuring local seafood, from F90 to F250. 17 rooms. Restaurant closed Tuesday except during July and August.

29150 Châteaulin

HOTEL AU BON ACCUEIL
Port Launay
☎ (98) 86 15 77
Châteaulin in southern Finistère is a delightful spot famous for salmon fishing, set between coast and country, and the Hôtel au Bon Accueil is a good place in which to stay. Quite large for a *logis*, with 55 rooms, it offers good menus, with local salmon when in season, at prices from F56 to F175. Restaurant closed Sunday evening and Monday.

LE NICOLAS
Near the church
☎ (98) 86 05 64
This small restaurant in the town centre is a family business, popular with the local people, and offers traditional food at moderate prices. Menus from F55 to F125. Well worth a visit.

35270 Combourg

HOTEL DU CHATEAU ET DES VOYAGEURS
1 Place Chateaubriand
☎ (99) 73 00 38
The Hôtel du Château at Combourg, south of St Malo, is a fairly large hotel with what one correspondent has described as 'one of the finest restaurants I have found in this part of Brittany'. The service is excellent, the food first-class and there are menus at prices for all pockets from F77 to F250. 30 rooms. Restaurant closed Sunday evening in summer.

29110 Concarneau

HOTEL DES SABLES BLANCS
Plage des Sables Blancs
☎ (98) 97 01 39
M. Chabrier's hotel by the beach near Concarneau has 48 rooms and a good range of fine menus from F60 to F170. As one might expect in this major fishing port of Finistère, the seafood is excellent.

TY MAD
Off Avenue Pierre-Gaugin
☎ (98) 97 00 60
The name drew me in to this family restaurant, where it took hours to work my way through a vast *plateau de fruits de mer*. Well known in

Concarneau and very popular with the locals, this place is not to be missed.

44490 Le Croisic

HOTEL LES NIDS
Plage de Port
☎ (40) 23 00 63
Le Croisic is a fascinating little port on the Loire estuary in the south of Brittany. Les Nids has 28 rooms and good menus at prices from F90 to F250. Very pleasant garden, the ideal place to dine on a summer evening.

122100 Dinan

HOTEL LE D'AVAUGOUR
1 Place du Champ-Clos
☎ (96) 39 07 49
This highly-recommended 3-star *logis*, right in the centre of Dir in, lies opposite the equestrian statue of Bertrand du Guesclin, the local hero. It is a marvellous hotel, serving excellent food on menus from F100 to F170. 27 rooms.

LA CARAVELLE
14 Place Duclos
☎ (96) 39 00 11
Seafood is the speciality of this excellent restaurant, which holds a Michelin rosette and a loyal clientele. Try the *homard rôti au beurre salé*. Not cheap. Prices from F200 to F350.

LE DUGUESCLIN
9 Rue Ste Claire
☎ Not available
A good meal at this small, attractive restaurant need cost no more than F50, although there is a wide choice of menus from F40 to F200. Many dishes are grilled over an open wood fire in the restaurant. Friendly staff and a good wine list.

56120 Josselin

HOTEL DU CHATEAU
1 Rue de Général de Gaulle
☎ (97) 22 20 11
A good 2-star *logis*, close to the famous castle of the Dukes of Rohan. 36 rooms. Menus in the attractive restaurant from F65 to F165.

HOTEL DE FRANCE
Place Notre Dame
☎ (97) 22 23 06
A highly recommended little hotel-restaurant, where you can rely on the food being beautifully cooked and carefully served. Menus from F55 to F150.

22300 Lannion

HOTEL DE LA PLAGE
St Michel-en-Grève
☎ (96) 35 74 43
Runner-up in the Brittany Ferries Restaurant Competition, this hotel is actually by the beach at St Michel, 6 miles from Lannion on the north coast of Brittany. A delightful dining room with fresh flowes on every table, and good value from the F75 menu, which offered a choice of eight dishes for every course.

56550 Locoal-Mendon

LE MANOIR DE POHR-KERIO
Pohr-Kerio
Morbihan ·
☎ (97) 24 67 57
This restaurant which won the Brittany Ferries Competition in 1988 is deep in the country and not the easiest place to find. A beautiful manor house off the L'Orient-to-Vannes road, it offers menus from F70 to F105, a small price to pay for first-class food. Try *médaillons de lotte*, the *filet de porc*, or the strawberry soup. The food is a touch *nouvelle*, but the portions are more than adequate. Well worth the search.

35400 St Malo

A L'ABORDAGE
5 Place Poissonnerie
☎ Not available
A small, first-floor restaurant overlooking the square containing the fish market in the town centre. Try the excellent seafood platter with a bottle of *cidre-bouché*. Menus from F120 to F250. Closed Monday.

AU GAI BEC
4 Rue des Lauriers
☎ Not available
A runner-up in the Brittany Ferries Competition, this restaurant has some English-speaking staff, good food and very keen prices with a good meal from about F60.

HOTEL CENTRAL
6 Grande Rue
☎ (99) 40 87 70
This pleasant hotel in the main street inside the *intra muros* of St Malo is one of the more traditional type of restaurant, with staff in white aprons and discreet music. Not cheap, with menus from F100 to F200, but excellent value.

HOTEL DE LA PORTE ST PIERRE
2 Place du Guet
☎ (99) 40 91 27
The little walled town of St Malo has several *logis* and many good restaurants. This 2-star *logis* has 25 rooms and a good range of local menus featuring seafood and galettes and ranging from F55 to F200. Restaurant closed Tuesday.

29223 St Thégonnec

AUBERGE ST THEGONNEC
6 Place de la Mairie
☎ (98) 79 61 18
This tiny six-room *logis*, just opposite the famous *parish-clos* of St Thégonnec is the ideal centre for touring the calvaries of northern Finistère. M. Le Coz serves good Breton food in his charming restaurant and has maintained high standards for many years. Menus from F49 to F130. Restaurant closed Monday, except during July and August.

56000 Vannes

L'AUBERGES DE PETIT VERGER
Corn-er-Hoet
Monterblanc
☎ (97) 45 95 57
The Petit Verger has maintained a high standard of food and wine for many years and continues to devise excellent dishes. Try the *blanquette d'escargot* or the *truite mousseline* from the F80 menu.

HOTEL LE TY LANN
11 Rue Joseph Le Brix
St Ave
☎ (97) 60 71 79
This little hotel at St Ave, 3 miles from the walled city of Vannes, is an ideal centre for exploring the Gulf of the Morbihan. Good food, carefully prepared and presented, with menus from F69 to F160. 18 rooms. Restaurant closed Saturday and Sunday evenings outside the high season.

3550 Vitré

HOTEL DU PETIT-BILLOT
5 Place Maréchal Leclerc
☎ (99) 75 02 10
Mme Lancelot runs this comfortable French hotel on traditional lines, and her husband cooks traditional value-for-money French meals at prices from F50 to F100. 23 rooms. Restaurant closed Friday evening and Saturday except during July and August.

CHAMPAGNE-ARDENNES

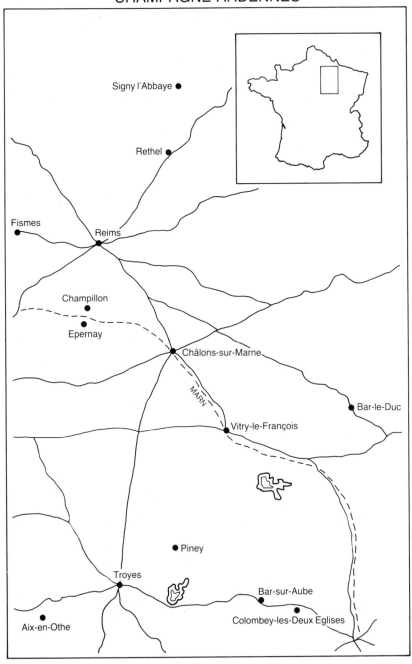

Signy l'Abbaye ●

Rethel ●

Fismes ●

Reims ●

Champillon ●

Epernay ●

Châlons-sur-Marne ●

MARN

Bar-le-Duc ●

Vitry-le-François ●

Piney ●

Troyes ●

Bar-sur-Aube ●

Colombey-les-Deux Eglises ●

Aix-en-Othe ●

CHAMPAGNE-
ARDENNES

I owe a great debt to Champagne, or more particularly to the city of
Reims, for it was here, in my mid-thirties, that I changed my mind
about France and the French. This event, a secular version of St
Paul's encounter on the Road to Damascus, occurred one October
night many years ago when I was returning to England by car from
the Frankfurt Book Fair. I had somehow got lost trying to find
Belgium and, horror of horrors, ended up in France where, as everyone then knew, the English were unpopular and the locals no better
than they should be. It was also widely believed at the time that the
only way you could afford to travel in France was by throwing your
life's savings ashore from the ferry and then staying on board.
However, I could drive no further and therefore dragged myself
gloomily into the Hôtel Foch in Reims – I can see the neon sign now.
In the end I stayed four days in Reims, and why not? The room was
comfortable, the water hot, the people smiling and the prices low,
and all those horror stories quite without foundation. I also visited
Epernay, where the Relais de Royal Champagne on the hill produced
a half-bottle of the local vintage free with every meal. I then explored
the champagne caves of Reims, and left a total convert. The rest, as
they say, is history.

Any visitor to this part of France should head at once for Reims, a
very fine town of great antiquity. The kings of France were crowned
in the cathedral here, and it remains a famous place, although the

real centre for champagne is actually Epernay, which although much smaller is actually set among the vineyards. The houses and streets of Reims stand on countless miles of cellars, some 15 miles in all, dug out of the chalk and filled with millions of bottles of champagne. Champagne is said to have originated at Ay, and all visitors should see the Abbey at Hautvillers where Dom Pérignon discovered how to keep the bubbles in the bottle. Days can be spent hereabouts visiting the cellars of the champagne shippers and since every visit concludes with a tasting, this can be no bad thing. The vineyards lie on the banks of the River Marne, which flows through Epernay, and the whole area is buttressed by that chalk strata which provides the cellars and emerges further west at Cap Gris-Nez on the Channel Coast.

The region of Champagne-Ardennes now consists of four *départements* – Ardennes, Marne, Haute-Marne and Aube – which together create a rectangular region running north–south from the Belgian frontier to the border with Burgundy. The countryside is varied but the name Champagne comes from the Latin word *camparis*, or flat-land, and most of the land is gentle and rolling. To the east lie the hills and the woods of the Ardennes, through which the German Army debouched onto the aforesaid plain in 1940 and again during the Battle of the Bulge, in 1944. The Ardennes was once one vast forest, and although the woods are much reduced, it is still a great woodland wilderness, a paradise for birds and deer and wild boar. During the Middle Ages Champagne was one of the richest provinces of France, not from the wine but from the great trade fairs which were held here, at Troyes and Bar-sur-Aube, which drew merchants from all corners of Christendom. The two areas offer a contrast of terrain, the chalk slopes of open vineyards and the fields of Champagne contrasting vividly with the steep hills and woods of the Ardennes. The best time to visit this region is in the autumn, when the vintage is coming in and the woods are aflame with the turning leaf, but there is always a lot to see and do hereabouts in some very fine and historic towns and cities. Apart from Reims, the main towns are Epernay, Châlons-sur-Marne, which is seamed by canals, and Troyes, which has a very fine medieval centre and the Church of St John, where Henry V of England married Catherine of Valois in 1420.

Among the smaller places, the traveller's eye will be drawn to the great double-armed cross of Lorraine which overtops the village of Colombey-les-Deux-Eglises, once the home and now the burial place of General Charles de Gaulle. Chaumont, in the Haute-Marne, has a splendid railway viaduct, and history buffs will probably enjoy a visit to Sedan in the Ardennes, where Napoleon III was trounced by the

Prussians during the Franco-Prussian War of 1870. Wine-buffs will venerate Ste Ménehould, not least because Dom Pérignon was born here in 1715. All in all, this is a region for travellers who enjoy fine towns, good food and the best wine in the world.

Essential sights

Bar-sur-Aube, Chaumont, Colombey-les-Deux-Eglises, Laon, a fine cathedral city still encircled by 3 miles of curtain wall, Soissons, Troyes and, of course, Epernay and Reims.

Food

As one might expect, the restaurateurs of Champagne have risen to meet the expectations raised by the presence of the 'Queen of Wines' and the cooking of the area is to a very high standard, without drawing on local recipes to any great degree. In the Ardennes, the northern influence is strong, the food not unlike that of the Nord, or Belgium – you can get *waterzooi* for example. Among cold meats, hams – indeed all *charcuterie* – are very popular, and the Ardennes forests produce venison and *sanglier* (wild boar) in a wide variety of forms, in stews, pies, pâtés and hams. Ardennes ham, smoked to a deep red, is quite delicious and among other local specialities the *pieds-de-cochon* – pigs' trotters – from Ste Ménehould, and the *coq à la bière*, chicken in beer, are both delicious. The area is also noted for *pave* – turkey – which is served all year in these parts and not, as in England, just at Christmas. For a great dish on a cold day try *potée champenoise*, a delicious ham, bacon and cabbage soup or stew. For a good local cheese try the *carré de l'Est*, a square-shaped cow's milk cheese, as well as *caprice de Dieu*, *chaumont* and *centre de Champagne*. Reims produces excellent macaroons. When 'champagne' is used in cooking it is usually the unfermented wine.

Wine

The wine is, of course, Champagne. Champagne is the wine that is said to go with everything, while managing perfectly well on its own. Only wines from this area, produced from the grapes growing in specially designated fields, may be called champagne, and the local *vignerons* currently produce about 120,000,000 bottles a year, as well as some good still white and red wines. Most of the latter are drunk locally. The creation of champagne is credited to a Benedictine monk, Dom Pérignon of Ste Ménehould, who discovered that a second fermentation could be induced to a wine by adding a *tirage*, a mixture of sugar and yeast that adds the sparkle and the bubbles. The process is explained and demonstrated by the guides who conduct visitors on tours through the cellars beneath the streets of Reims. Here you can choose from a host of famous names, and although my favourite is Veuve Clicquot, there are those who prefer Krug, Moët et Chandon, or Mumm, among others. As to the particular taste, there is *brut zéro* (totally dry), *brut* (very very dry), *très sec* (very dry), *extra-sec* (dry), *sec* (not too dry), *demi-sec* (quite sweet), and *doux* (very sweet). All champagnes are blended, and a good champagne will be at its peak six to twelve years after the vintage.

Strangely enough, not everyone likes champagne, but the area does produce some excellent reds, so try those from Bouzy (delightful name), Vertus or Cimières, or, since we are still in northern France, one of the local beers. For an aperitif try *ratafia de Champagne*, a mix of cognac and white wine.

RESTAURANTS

10160 Aix-en-Othe

AUBERGE DE LA SCIERIE
La Vove
☎ (25) 46 71 26
Aix lies south of the N60, halfway between Troyes and Sens, the ideal spot for touring into Northern Burgundy or the Aube. M. Lefort has 14 rooms and a very good restaurant, with menus from F108 to F195. Well worth a diversion. Restaurant closed Monday evening and Tuesday.

10200 Bar-sur-Aube

HOSTELLERIE DE LA CHAUMIERE
Arsonval
☎ (25) 26 11 02
Actually 4 miles north-west of Bar-sur-Aube, on the RN19 to Troyes, this little country restaurant serves very good food at a leisurely pace and provides the perfect lunchtime stop, or a good evening meal. Only three rooms. Menus from F85 to F210. Closed Sunday evening and Monday.

55000 Bar-le-Duc

HOTEL DE LA GARE
Place de la République
☎ (29) 79 01 45
Close to the battlefields of the Great War, the *Guerre de Quatorze*, Bar-le-Duc is a rugged little place. This 2-star *logis* has 35 rooms and a very good restaurant with menus from F60 to F100. Not fine fare, but good, reliable cooking. Cyclists will enjoy Bar-le-Duc, where the bicycle was invented by the brothers Michaux.

MEUSE GOURMANDE
1 Rue François de Guise
☎ (29) 79 28 40
Set in the old town, the Ville-Haute, overlooking the Marne, this small restaurant has a name to uphold. It does so very well, with good food featuring local dishes, and a very fine wine list. Only a few tables, so book.

51000 Châlons-sur-Marne

HOTEL L'ANGLETERRE
19 Place M. Tissier
☎ (26) 68 21 51
The Restaurant Jacky Michel in this small but very attractive hotel has a Michelin rosette, so the chef will not easily succumb to pleas for too solid food. Not cheap, with menus from F150 to F350, but marvellous quality. Try the *pot au feu de foie gras aux nouilles fraîches*. This is *the* place to eat in Châlons and worth a diversion. Excellent wine list. Best to book.

51160 Champillon

LE ROYAL CHAMPAGNE
Outside village
☎ (26) 52 87 11
This hotel-restaurant, while not cheap, is the great restaurant of the Epernay region, and set on a hill overlooking the vineyards. A Michelin rosette, dishes like *turbot à la Montardi*, and a friendly, far from snooty staff, make a visit to this restaurant a delight. 25 rooms. Menus from F300 to F350.

52330 Colombey-les-Deux-Eglises

AUBERGE DE LA MONTAGNE
☎ (25) 01 51 69
It is more than probable that anyone driving across the Haute-Marne
will divert into Colombey, the home of General de Gaulle. If so, this
auberge has 9 rooms and very adequate food. Restaurant closed
Monday evening and Tuesday, except from June to 1 September.

51200 Epernay

LE MANOIR DE CHAMPAGNE
19 Ave Champagne
☎ (26) 55 04 45
This excellent restaurant lies in the centre of Epernay, close to the
wine caves, and serves excellent food from a range of menus, priced
from F125 to F200. Closed Wednesday.

51170 Fismes

HOTEL LA BOULE D'OR
Route de Laon
☎ (26) 78 11 24
This tiny 7-room *logis* in the Marne is noted for its food, and M.
Blanquet won the Regional Cookery Competition with his *charlotte
de grenouilles aux fine herbes et au beurre champenoise*. . . . There
cannot be many recipes which begin with 'Take a kilogram of frogs'
legs'! Menus from F70 to F195. Restaurant closed Sunday evening
and Monday.

110220 Piney

LE VIEUX LOGIS
Brévonnes
☎ (25) 46 30 17
M. Baudesson writes, 'Le Vieux Logis is a big, typical cottage of
Champagne, dating from 1790 but entirely restored by me. I prepare
cooking with regional products, and since 1984 I have been carrying
off the first prize.' Try the *mignardaise de volaille champenoise*,
boned, stuffed chicken with Champagne cream sauce. Menus from
F54 to F160. 7 rooms. Restaurant closed Sunday evening and
Monday.

08300 Rethel

LE MODERNE
Place de la Gare
☎ (24) 38 44 54
This is the *logis* hotel that gets into all the guides, mainly because of
the food. The dining room is simple but very neat and the menu
features local specialities. Try the *rillettes de champagne*. 23 rooms.
Menus from F69 to F240.

LE SANGLIER DES ARDENNES
1 Rue P. Curie
☎ (24) 38 45 19
A good 2-star *logis* with a fascinating name, good food and pleasant
staff. Menus from F58 to F98. 24 rooms. Closed Sunday.

51100 Reims

LE CHARDONNAY
184 Ave d'Epernay
☎ (26) 06 08 60
Though not cheap, with dinner starting at F230, this attractive
restaurant set in an old farmhouse is well worth a visit. Try the
crevettes au vinaigre vin de champagne. Closed Saturday lunchtime
and Sunday.

LE CONTINENTAL
95 Place Drouet-d'Erlon
☎ (26) 47 01 47
M. Lantenois runs a tight, happy ship in this traditional restaurant,
with menus from F76 to F300, and the *carte* offering excellent value.

HOTEL AU TAMBOUR
63 Rue de Magneux
☎ (26) 40 59 22
Reims is full of hotels and restaurants but a little short of *logis*, with
just this one to carry the flag. 14 rooms, and a pleasant restaurant
serving local food. Menus from F55 to F120. Restaurant closed Saturday midday and Sunday evening.

LE VIGNERON
Place Paul Jarnot
☎ (26) 47 00 71
Close to the cathedral, this little bistro is a poem to the wines of
Champagne, and the food that goes with them. A vast selection of
champagnes and excellent cooking make Le Vigneron a must. Expect
to pay about F200 per head.

08460 Signy l'Abbaye

AUBERGE DE L'ABBAYE
Près des Vieilles Arcades
☎ (24) 52 81 27
Signy, north of Rethel, lost its abbey in 1789, but this lovely village is the ideal centre for exploring the forests of the Ardennes. Only 12 rooms, but a splendid restaurant run by Mme Léfebvre, where the menus change daily. Try such local dishes as *jambon d'Ardennes* or *truite Val de Vence*. Menu prices from F60 to F120. Closed Wednesday evening and Friday from 9 pm.

10000 Troyes

LE CHAMPAGNE
4 Ave de Maréchal Joffre
☎ (25) 79 90 90
Troyes is usually overwhelmed by historic Reims, but is still a very fine town. This restaurant, in a setting of considerable splendour, offers very good food indeed. Expect to pay F200 per head.

LE ST VINCENT
Gare de Troyes
☎ (25) 73 16 01
One of the old rules for travellers in France was, if all else fails, try the station buffet, where they often serve good food. This is certainly the case in Troyes. Good, solid, well-cooked fare is served under the usual bright lights, but you can park and the service is swift and friendly.

151300 Vitry-le-François

HOTEL DE LA CLOCHE
34 Rue Aristide Briand
☎ (26) 74 03 84
Vitry is a pleasant town of the Marne, with this fine 2-star *logis*. 22 rooms. The restaurant offers local dishes and good wine on menus from F85 to F105. Restaurant closed Sunday evening.

ALSACE, LORRAINE AND THE VOSGES

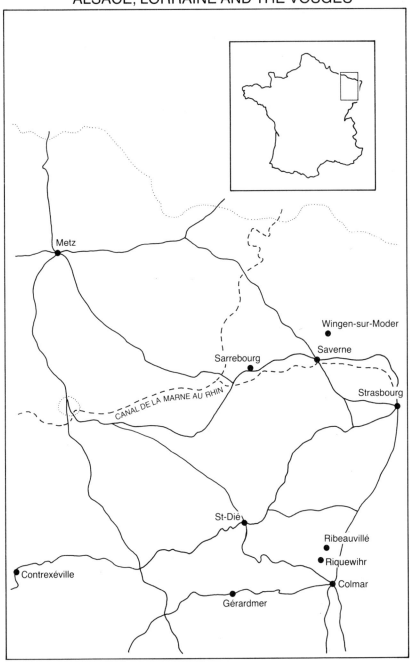

ALSACE, LORRAINE AND THE VOSGES

The twin provinces of Alsace and Lorraine, on the eastern frontier of France and linked by the hills and forests of the Vosges, have enjoyed, or endured, a rather chequered history, with their ownership hotly contested by France and Germany until as recently as 1945, when, after centuries of conflict, both provinces were finally reunited with France. Even so, and despite the fact that Lorraine was the birthplace of that French heroine, Joan of Arc, both provinces retain a distinctly Germanic tinge, which is most noticeable in the place-names and the food, although the old quarrels are most deeply marked in the north of Lorraine, on the scarred 1916 battlefield of Verdun.

Lorraine is largely occupied by a plateau, a gently rolling country-side of fields and woods and orchards, although the north of the plateau is largely devoted to the production of iron and steel and coal mining, a once rich inheritance that aroused the envy of the Germans and led to frequent annexations. The Vosges are delightful hills, more gentle on their western slopes, rising as the spine of the hills moves south, yet nowhere higher than 4300 ft (1425 m), and therefore a paradise for summer walkers and cross-country skiers during the long, hard winters. To the east the Vosges fall away sharply onto the plain of Alsace, with rich vineyards along the lower slopes of the hills, which are studded with mighty castles and small villages, beyond which the plain runs out to the Rhine.

The three regions of Alsace, Lorraine and the Vosges together comprise six *départements*: Meuse, Moselle, Meurthe-et-Moselle, Vosges, Bas-Rhin and Haut-Rhin, these last two bounded on the east by the Rhine, beyond which lies the Black Forest of Germany. This is a very diverse region, with a variety of terrain. There are areas, such as the Vosges or the Crêtes (the 'Crests') which will attract the country lover, the walker, the birdwatcher, the wine buff. There are various *Routes* through these hills and countryside, so follow the *Route des Vins* or the *Route des Crêtes*, which take travellers into areas which first-time visitors might otherwise miss.

Places which should feature on any traveller's itinerary include the Ballon d'Alsace in the south of the Vosges, which is a 3750-ft (1250 m) peak, giving a marvellous view of the surrounding countryside. Colmar should not be missed and a visit here should take on the Musée d'Unterlinden, which contains Grünewald's magnificent *Isenheim Altar* – note those Germanic names. Any Francophile will make a pilgrimage to the tiny village of Domrémy, birthplace of Joan of Arc, which is why it is now called Domrémy-la-Pucelle ('the Maid'). Her cottage home is now a museum and a good side trip from here would be to the castle at Vaucouleurs, whose captain, Robert de Baudricourt, sent the Maid to see the Dauphin at Chinon. Those who like sports will enjoy the resort of Gérardmer in the Vosges. Others might press on up the chain to the shattered countryside around the 1916 battlefield of Verdun. There is a huge combined ossuary and memorial on the battlefield, and parts of the old trench systems and the old forts have been retained. I cannot pretend that Verdun is a cheerful place, but students of European history can hardly give it a miss.

Alsace in particular is beautiful, the towns as much as the country. Before I first saw the area I was reluctant to go, feeling that Alsace was hardly France at all, and perhaps too Germanic for my taste. It certainly looks different from other parts of France, though not unlike parts of Burgundy. The medieval towns are full of half-timbered houses with colourful glazed-tile roofs, lots of flowers line the balconies and window-boxes, and the streets are cobbled. I can think of few towns in France as beautiful as Colmar, or more of a surprise than Strasbourg, which reveals itself as a splendid city, with canals running everywhere. Few castles can be as magnificent as Haut-Koenigsbourg in the Bas-Rhin *département* to the north, and few towns as interesting as the wine town of Kayserberg in the Haut-Rhin further south. Riquewihr is a wine town of Alsace, very beautiful, rather small, and vies with Ribeauvillé for the title of the most interesting place in the area for committed wine buffs. My personal choice would be Obernai in the Bas-Rhin which, apart from Colmar, is my favourite town in the entire region.

Towns are important hereabouts, for except in the depths of winter, the weather is fickle and inclined to be dreary, especially in Lorraine. On wet days the towns are useful, for they all contain museums and little shops set along cobbled streets and, of course, many good restaurants. Apart from the time of the vintage in the autumn, this is not really a tourist region, which is why I would urge all true travellers to go there and tour by car, cycle or on foot, perhaps through the Vosges, along one of the footpath trails of the *Grande Randonée*, or on one of the local footpaths waymarked by that excellent institution, the Club Vosgian. It is worth repeating that this part of France is really beautiful and, industry apart, quite unspoiled. It has good wine and great food, fascinating towns, and a great variety of scenery. If you are seeking somewhere new to visit in France, then Alsace, Lorraine and the beautiful Vosges could be just the place to choose.

Essential sights

Follow the *Route des Vins* and the *Route des Crêtes*. The Ballon d'Alsace offers tremendous views. Among towns, Colmar, Nancy, very elegant; Obernai, Riquewihr and Ribeauvillé, essential stops. Strasbourg is the capital of Alsace, with a magnificent cathedral and many canals. The northern Vosges is now a National Park, well worth visiting, and history lovers should visit Haut-Koenigsbourg, parts of which date from before 1490, and the battlefield of Verdun.

Food

The local food, like the place-names, has a distinctly Germanic touch, particularly in Alsace. The great dish of Alsace is *choucroute*, better known perhaps as *Sauerkraut*, or pickled cabbage, but much nicer than the German variety. Other popular dishes found in most restaurants include *kassler*, which is smoked pork, or *Leberknödeln*, liver dumplings. Any dish made *à l'Alsacienne* comes with cabbage and onions, perhaps with sausages. In the Vosges, *sanglier* (wild boar) is often available, with the local speciality, *marcassin* (young boar) on offer during the winter months, a great dish after a day on cross-country skis. In the west, *quiche lorraine*, an egg and bacon flan, is available everywhere, and with the *foie gras* of Strasbourg provides the region's great contribution to world gastronomy. But the locals rave about *tarte flambé*, eggs, bacon and onions, with not too much pastry – quite delicious. Strasbourg is famous for *foie gras* and on the whole the food hereabouts tends to be of the ample, rich, rib-sticking variety. The cheeseboard is dominated by Münster, which has a good, pungent nose to it and may not be to everyone's taste. St Rémy and Gérardmer cheeses are milder and perhaps more appealing. All the local cheese is made from cow's milk and the local puddings tend to be rich, sweet and heavy.

Wine

The great drink of the entire region is probably lager beer, which the locals consume in vast quantities. The wines of Alsace are differentiated not by area or château but by grape variety: Riesling, Tokay, Muscat, Gewürztraminer, Sylvaner. Most of the local wines are white and AC, though there is a certain amount of Pinot Noir rosé. They tend to be strong (12°–14°), with a range of taste from the dry Riesling to a fruity Muscat. The best dry white wines are the Riesling and Sylvaner, especially that from Riquewihr in Alsace. In Lorraine, the best wines are Moselle and the Côtes de Toul, although there is also a pleasant dry rosé from Toul – *gris de gris*. There is also a wide range of powerful liqueurs and *eaux de vie*: Kirsch, *framboise* (raspberry), *mirabelle* (plum brandy), and many more. Those who don't like alcohol can drink the waters of Vittel.

RESTAURANTS

88540 Bussang

HOTEL DES DEUX CLEFS
Village centre
☎ (29) 61 51 01
This hotel, run by Mme Fritz, has a Regional Cooking sign, 15 rooms and good, inexpensive menus from F55 to F100. Also a good wine list. Worth a detour. Restaurant closed saturday.

HOTEL DU TREMPLIN
Rue de IIIème RTA
☎ (29) 61 50 30
Another little town with three good *logis*, Bussang is ideal for exploring the southern Vosges, and is at no great distance from the Grand Ballon. M. Gabriel won the regional context for Lorraine in 1987, and

maintains a high standard in mainly local cuisine. 20 rooms. Menus from F55 to F130. Restaurant closed Monday.

68000 Colmar

HOTEL BEAUSEJOUR
25 Rue du Ladhof
☎ (89) 41 37 16
Colmar is probably the prettiest town in eastern France and *must* be visited. The Beauséjour serves excellent local dishes in a pleasant dining room, with menus from F75 to F160. 29 rooms. Restaurant closed at lunchtime on Saturday, Sunday and Monday.

HOTEL MAJESTIC
1 Rue de la Gare
☎ (89) 41 45 19
The Majestic, near the station, serves menus with local dishes. Menus from F60 to F150. 40 rooms. Restaurant closed Sunday and Monday evening.

88140 Contrexéville

HOTEL DE FRANCE
58 Ave du Roi Stanislas
☎ (29) 08 04 13
Contrexéville has three *logis* and some good restaurants. The town is close to the village of Domrémy-la-Pucelle, where Joan of Arc was born, probably in 1412. This hotel has 40 rooms, and menus from F75 to F180.

88100 St-Dié

LE HAUT FER
Rougiville
☎ (29) 55 03 48
This little hotel of the Vosges lies in a hamlet south-east of St-Dié. A pleasant *logis* with 16 rooms and menus from F80 to F180. Restaurant closed Sunday evening and Monday.

LE TATRAS
4 Rue d'Hellieule
☎ (29) 56 10 12
This pretty restaurant serves the most excellent food, including such rich dishes as *saumon et sandre aux deux sauces*. Good wine list and very well-chosen menus. Not cheap, with menus from F80 to F300, but well worth it. Best to book.

88400 Gérardmer

AUBERGE DES DEUX ETANGS
Col de Martimpré
☎ (29) 63 14 31
This little *logis* – 11 rooms – lies on a hill outside the resort of Gérardmer, popular with summer walkers and skiers in winter. Regional food at reasonable prices; menus from F60 to F150. Good wine list. Restaurant closed Monday outside July and August.

AU GRAND CERF
Place du Tilleul
☎ (29) 63 06 31
A pleasant dining room looking out to the gardens and the hills of the Vosges makes this restaurant a good place to dine, even without the good food. A *gastronomique* menu at around F300, but several others, perfectly adequate, between F80 and F170.

68720 Illfurth

AUBERGE DE FROENINGEN
Route d'Illfurth
Fröeningen
☎ (89) 25 48 48
This little village in Haut-Rhin has this excellent, 3-star *logis*, a typical *auberge* of Alsace, beautifully furnished and just 4 miles from Mulhouse. This is one of those elegant *logis*, and Jean-Marie Renner and his son in the kitchen, with his daughter in the dining room, make an efficient and friendly team. *Foie gras, cassoulette d'escargots au Riesling*, and *matelote de grenouilles à l'ail*, are just a few of the excellent dishes. Only seven rooms. Menus from F100 to F265. Well worth a detour but best to book.

57000 Metz

LA DINANDERIE
2 Rue de Paris
☎ (87) 30 14 40
One advantage of industrial towns is that good restaurants abound, as here, where Marthe Piergiorgi offers menus from F160 to F195, and good wine list. Restaurant closed Sunday and Monday.

HOTEL LUTECE
11 Rue de Paris
☎ (87) 30 27 25
Unlike the other *logis* in Metz, the Lutèce has a dining room, as well

as 20 rooms, and offers a warm welcome. Not luxurious, but perfectly adequate for touring this part of France. Menus from F50 to F95. Restaurant closed Saturday and Sunday.

68150 Ribeauvillé

HOTEL AU CHEVAL BLANC
122 Grande Rue
☎ (89) 73 61 38
Not the largest hotel in town, with just 25 rooms, but the restaurant does serve regional cuisine and has a well-chosen range of good menus, reasonably priced between F50 and F140. Restaurant closed Monday.

RESTAURANT DES VOSGES
2 Grande Rue
☎ (89) 73 61 39
This is an hotel, only 17 rooms in a large building, but noted locally for the restaurant, and perhaps most of all for the wine cellar. Menus from F150 to F350. Try the *mosaïque de ris de veau* – delicious. Restaurant closed Monday and Tuesday lunchtime.

68340 Riquewihr

LE SARMENT D'OR
4 Rue du Cerf
☎ (89) 47 92 85
This little wine town *must* be visited on any tour of Haut-Rhin, so while in the area stay at this fine little *logis*, which serves good regional food and has a fine cellar. Menus from F79 to F199. 10 rooms, so it is best to book. Restaurant closed Sunday evening and Monday.

57000 Sarrebourg

HOTEL DE FRANCE
3 Ave de France
☎ (87) 03 21 47
Sarrebourg is one of the chief attractions of the Moselle, so while in the region stay here, at this large 30-room *logis*, where the restaurant serves good, well-prepared local dishes. Menus from F65 to F150. Restaurant closed Saturday and Sunday evening.

67700 Saverne

HOTEL FISCHER
15 Rue de la Gare
☎ (88) 91 19 53
It is hard to imagine anyone visiting Bas-Rhin without visiting Saverne, which has the castle of the Prince-Bishops of Strasbourg and easy access to the country around Dabo, a beautiful part of the region. This excellent *logis* has 19 rooms, local dishes and a high reputation. Moderate prices, with menus from F50 to F140. Restaurant closed Friday evening and Saturday.

67000 Strasbourg

HOTEL AU CERF D'OR
6 Place de l'Hôpital
☎ (88) 36 20 05
Strasbourg is a splendid city, full of canals and fine buildings, and as the seat of the European Parliament frequently crowded, so it is best to book bed and board. This hotel has only 16 rooms but the restaurant serves local dishes from a range of menus priced from F50 to F150. Restaurant closed Wednesday evening.

RESTAURANT CROCODILE
10 Rue Outré
☎ (88) 32 13 02
Strasbourg is a place where a first-class meal should round off any visit. This restaurant has two Michelin rosettes and excellent food. Try the *gratin de langouste*. Not cheap – estimate F300 per head – and booking essential. Closed Sunday and Monday.

67290 Wingen-sur-Moder

LA CLAIRIERE
Route d'Inguilleur
La Petite-Pierre
☎ (88) 70 47 76
This hotel in La Petite-Pierre possesses a Regional Cooking 'saucepan'. 19 rooms and a very good restaurant. Menus from F67 to F200.

HOTEL AU LION D'OR
15 Rue Principale
La Petite-Pierre
☎ (88) 70 45 06
This little town, or large village, in Bas-Rhin, north-east of Strasbourg, has only 640 inhabitants but no less than five 2-star *logis*,

more than you will find in many large towns. M. Robert Vellen of the Lion d'Or won the Regional Cookery Contest with his *civet de chevreuil*, and his *sanglier chasseur*, from a menu replete with local dishes. 35 rooms, menus from F75 to F260. Very good value. Restaurant closed Wednesday evening and Thursday.

ILE DE FRANCE

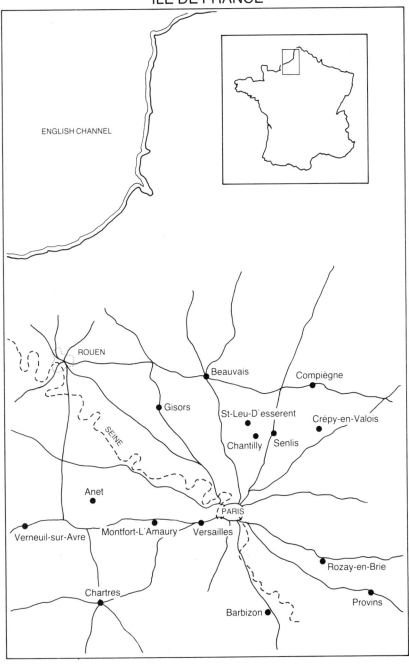

ENGLISH CHANNEL

ROUEN

Beauvais

Compiègne

Gisors

St-Leu-D'esserent

Crépy-en-Valois

SEINE

Chantilly   Senlis

Anet

PARIS

Verneuil-sur-Avre   Montfort-L'Amaury   Versailles

Rozay-en-Brie

Chartres

Provins

Barbizon

ILE DE FRANCE

Although this book concentrates on country hotels and restaurants, bypassing those of Paris, which would require a book on their own, as well as those in the larger provincial towns, it is still necessary to include the Ile de France, that broad stretch of countryside which enfolds and encircles the capital like a green scarf. The Ile de France is so called because it is bounded, like an island, on every side by rivers. This was the ancient demesne of the French kings, the place where they ruled directly, without the intervention of dukes and counts, and it therefore contains great palaces, such as Fontainebleau and Versailles, as well as the great country houses of the nobility, once attendant on the French Court, towns such as Anet, Vaux-le-Vicomte, Chantilly, Maintenon, and many other magnificent houses. The Ile de France is full of splendid sights and yet remains surprisingly neglected by foreign visitors who will rush south in their tens of thousands to see the châteaux of the Loire.

The Ile de France is a curious mixture of countryside and suburb, filling up fast with commuter towns and villages full of *maisons secondaires*, weekend retreats for the good, or at least rich, people of Paris. The dominating natural feature of the landscape is the great forests, once the royal hunting preserves, many of which, like the vast Forêt de Fontainebleau, are still full of deer and boar. Among all this green splendour, the traveller will find a great number of good hotels and splendid restaurants, so that a visit to the Ile de France will appeal in particular to those who enjoy good food (and are prepared to pay for it), and also to those who appreciate fine classical architecture. It is worth adding that the capital and the Ile de France

are encircled by a great, 800-mile long footpath, the GR1, but I think
it is safe to assume that most people touring the region will do so by
car.

Access is easy via any of the Channel ports, or via Charles de
Gaulle airport, which lies at Roissy-en-France, actually in the Ile de
France. My personal choice would be to enter the region from the
west, coming in across the Norman Vexin, stopping for the night at
Gisors, which has a good *logis* and a fine castle. From there, circling
the city in a clockwise direction, there are magnificent places to visit
every few miles. The modern Ile de France is formed from six
départements, excluding the two in the city. These are, clockwise from
the north, Oise, Seine-et-Marne, Essonne, Loir, Yvelines and Val
d'Oise. Leaving Gisors and heading east and north, a good route
would take in Mantes-la-Jolie in the Val d'Oise, which is not actually
very pretty but still notable as the place where William the Conqueror met his death by falling from his horse. Enghien-les-Bains is a
spa, and just to the north of it lies the first of many fine châteaux, at
Ecouen, built in the sixteenth century for the Constable of France,
Anne de Montmorency, who also built the even more splendid
example at Chantilly. Move north, through L'Isle Adam and stay a
day at Chantilly, perhaps to attend the races and certainly to see the
castle, which is full of treasures and quite beautiful. Note the stables,
which are magnificent because one of the past owners of Chantilly
believed in reincarnation and thought he would return to life as a
horse. The gardens here are by Le Nôtre, who also worked at Versailles and Vaux-le-Vicomte.

Further north lies Senlis, which has a fine cathedral, though not as
fine as that of Beauvais, capital of the Oise. After seeing Beauvais,
turn east to Compiègne, where Joan of Arc was captured in 1430. The
Palace of Compiègne looks drab on the outside, but the interior and
furnishings are quite magnificent. All the French kings from Louis
XIV on stayed at Compiègne, although it reached the heights of fame
in the last century when it was the favourite residence of Napoleon
III and his Empress Eugénie, in the years before the Franco-Prussian
War of 1870.

Heading south, along the eastern edge of Paris, there are more
great forests, and a fine little city at Meaux to visit before reaching
the medieval splendours of Provins and the famous château at Vaux-
le-Vicomte, which is the archetype of all the Ile de France châteaux.
All the great men of the age worked on Vaux when at the height of
their skills. Le Vau was the architect, Le Brun the decorator, Le
Nôtre the gardener, and Molière put on the play on the night the
château opened, to welcome Louis XIV and his Court. It was during
this event that the King suddenly realized that his Finance Minister,

Fouquet, had built Vaux with money filched from the royal coffers. Three weeks later Fouquet was in prison and his employees were working their wonders on the Sun King's great monument, the Palace of Versailles.

South of Vaux lies the Forêt de Fontainebleau, and the little riverside town of Moret-sur-Loing, one of my favourite places in the Ile de France. The Palace of Fontainebleau is much older than Versailles, having been built for François I in the early sixteenth century, and while it must be seen, the place to stay is at Barbizon in the forest, an artists' and writers' centre. From here cross into Yvelines to see Versailles, which will certainly take a full day, before heading down the valley for Chevreuse and the château at Rambouillet, the summer residence of the President of France. From here cross the Eure to see Anet, with a stop at Montfort-L'Amaury, the ancestral home of Simon de Montfort, father of the English parliament, and from here turn into Eure-et-Loire to visit Chartres.

This tour of the Ile de France will lead the traveller to some magnificent places and palaces, through a countryside which is still very quiet though very close to Paris and, of course, a visit to the *Ville Lumière* can always be included on a trip to the Ile de France.

Essential sights

Barbizon, the palaces of Fontainebleau, Versailles, Chantilly, and to the east, medieval Provins. Vaux-le-Vicomte is another marvellous place, and if only for the Cathedral, Chartres in Eure-et-Loir cannot be missed. Moret-sur-Loing is a little gem, while to go a little off the beaten track, try and visit Senlis, Rambouillet and Meaux.

Food and wine

The Ile de France, for all its other glories, cannot boast a regional cuisine. Nevertheless, you will eat as well here as in any other part of France, and among the multitude of local restaurants you will find all the cuisines from every part of France, with a wide choice of wines to match. There are, of course, some local products, like Brie from the pastures around Meaux, a town also famous for mustard. Dishes worth seeking out in the place of their birth include a pea soup, *potage St Germain*, and the range of dishes served with *sauce Bercy*, a sauce made with white wine and shallots. Those with a sweet tooth will enjoy the thick *crème Chantilly*, but in the main this is a region of fine cooking rather than specific local cuisine. There is, alas, no local wine.

RESTAURANTS

28260 Anet

AUBERGE DE LA ROSE
6 Rue Charles-Lechevrel
☎ (37) 41 90 64
Anet is a quiet little town in the Dreux forest, which contains the
beautiful château of Diane de Poitiers, mistress of Henri II. It also
contains this warm-hearted little *logis*, which has excellent menus,
from F83 to F235, with such dishes as *côte d'agneau anetaise*. 9 rooms.
Restaurant closed Sunday evening and Monday. Well worth a detour.

77630 Barbizon

LE BAS-BREAU
22 Grande Rue
☎ (1) 60 66 40 05
Far from cheap, but famous for its food, this restaurant ought to be
the place for that extra-special meal. Menus from F260 to F280; *à la
carte*, the sky's the limit.

HOSTELLERIE LA CLE D'OR
73 Grande Rue
☎ (1) 60 66 40 96
Barbizon is the ideal centre for touring the south of the Ile de France
and visiting Fontainebleau. An artists' and writers' town, it has
several good hotels but none better than this one, with 15 rooms and
menus from F135. Restaurant closed Sunday evening.

60000 Beauvais

RESTAURANT A LA COTELETTE
8 Rue des Jacobins
☎ (44) 45 04 42
Beauvais is sited strategically for British visitors heading for Paris
and has a cathedral magnificent enough to force a stop. At this
restaurant in the centre, there are two good menus from F150 and a
very full *carte*. Good service. Closed Sunday evening and Monday.

60500 Chantilly

RESTAURANT LES ETANGS
Coye-la-Forêt
☎ (44) 58 60 15
A very fine restaurant in the woods, five miles from Chantilly, with
an excellent F115 menu and a good cellar. Excellent for lunch. Closed
Monday evening and Tuesday.

LES QUATRE SAISONS
9 Ave du Général Leclerc
☎ (44) 57 04 65
The château of Chantilly cannot be missed on any tour of the Ile de
France, and you will eat well at this restaurant if you stick to the *petit
menu* at F95, or perhaps try the F135 menu. Good service, excellent
fish. Closed Sunday.

2800 Chartres

LA BLANQUETTE
45 Rue des Changes
☎ (37) 21 99 36
A delightful little restaurant, with M. Laviner's excellent food and
wine. Try the *blanquette de veau* if it is available. Menus from F62 to
F105. Closed Sunday evening.

HOTEL DE LA POSTE
3 Rue du Général Koenig
☎ (37) 21 04 27
Chartres is another necessary stop, to see the great cathedral, so
while there stay at this central 2-star *logis*, with 60 rooms. Although
it is one of the largest in France, it is still advisable to book. Menus
from F60 to F130.

60200 Compiègne

HOTEL DE FRANCE
17 Rue Eugène Floquet
☎ (44) 40 02 74
This *logis* has 20 rooms and a popular *rôtisserie*, Le Chat qui Tourne.
Menus from F108 to F170. A cheerful welcome, good food and an
excellent wine list.

◄──►

60800 Crépy-en-Valois

HOSTELLERIE DE GERESMES
1 Ave de l'Europe
☎ (44) 39 63 04
Little Crépy is a delightful little town east of Paris, and offers a warm welcome at this small 8-room *logis*. Menus from F80 to F210. Restaurant closed Sunday evening and Monday.

27140 Gisors

HOTEL MODERNE
Place de la Gare
☎ (32) 55 23 51
Gisors has a splendid castle, and was – or is – the capital of the Vexin, the border between Normandy and the Ile de France. A good nightstop for those people heading to or from Le Havre or Dieppe. This *logis* serves good country cooking. 31 rooms and menus from F50 to F100. Excellent value. Restaurant closed Sunday evening and Monday.

60340 St-Leu-Desserent

LE RELAIS ST DENIS
7 Rue l'Eglise
Villers-sous-St Leu
☎ (44) 56 31 87
M. and Mme Claude Bordinat won the 1987 Regional Logis Cookery Contest with their *St Jacques à la julienne d'anguille et petits légumes de Picardie*, which even sounds delicious. Mme Bordinat is a member of the National Association of Women Chefs, who are fairly rare, even in France, and their son works at La Tour d'Argent in Paris. Culinary skills seem to run in the family, so do not miss this pleasant little hotel-restaurant. *Menu gastronomique* from F180, *menu touristique* from F120. 9 rooms. Restaurant closed Sunday evening and Monday. Best to book.

78490 Montfort-L'Amaury

HOTEL DES VOYAGEURS
51 Rue de Paris
☎ (1) 34 86 00 14
Montfort was the birthplace of Simon de Montfort, Earl of Leicester, then a baron of the Ile de France. This is a good spot from which to explore the country south-west of Paris. 9 rooms and menus from F63 to F130. Restaurant closed Sunday evening and Monday.

◄──►

77160 Provins

HOSTELLERIE DE LA CROIX D'OR
1 Rue des Capucins
☎ (1) 64 00 01 96
This hotel has only six rooms, so it is the restaurant that brings in the money with its excellent menus from F80 to F210. Provins is a fine fortified town, east of Paris, that would not look out of place in the Dordogne. Don't miss it.

77540 Rozay-en-Brie

HOTEL DE FRANCE
84 Rue du Général Leclerc
☎ (1) 64 25 77 57
A small *logis* in a very pretty village, with an excellent reputation locally for good food. M. Gauthron's *barbue au ciche Seine-et-Marnais* won the *Logis de France* Regional Cookery Contest in 1987, and standards are high, with menus from F105 to F155. 10 rooms. Restaurant closed Wednesday. Rozay lies east of Paris on the N4, but the trip is worth it.

27130 Verneuil-sur-Avre

HOTEL DU SAUMON
89 Place de la Madeleine
☎ (32) 32 02 36
In 1424 Verneuil was the scene of a great battle between the English and a Franco-Scots army, which the English won. The town has few relics of those times, except a fine church and a big market square, which also contains this excellent *logis* with 28 rooms and a range of menus from F50 to F150.

60300 Senlis

AUBERGE DE FONTAINE
Fontaine-Chaalis
☎ (44) 54 20 22
Good country cooking is the speciality of this little 8-room *logis*, south-east of Senlis. That, plus the friendliness of M. Campion, make it worth a diversion. Menus from F100 to F175.

HOSTELLERIE DE LA PORTE-BELLON
51 Rue Bellon
☎ (44) 53 03 05
Senlis is a charming little town, a good centre for the northern Ile de

France, and this pleasant *logis* would make a good night-stop. 19 rooms. Menus from F98 to F250. Restaurant closed on Friday.

78000 Versailles

HOTEL DE LA CHASSE
2–4 Rue de la Chancellerie
☎ (1) 39 50 00 92
Versailles has many hotels but only one *logis* – this 2-star, 18-room hotel, with menus from F110 to F170. May be full in July/August, and it is always best to book.

LE POTAGER DU ROY
1 Rue Maréchal-Joffre
☎ (39) 50 35 34
This pleasant little restaurant, with menus from F150 to F250, offers excellent value and a fine selection of wines. Well worth a visit after a morning at the Palace. Closed Sunday and Monday.

WESTERN LOIRE

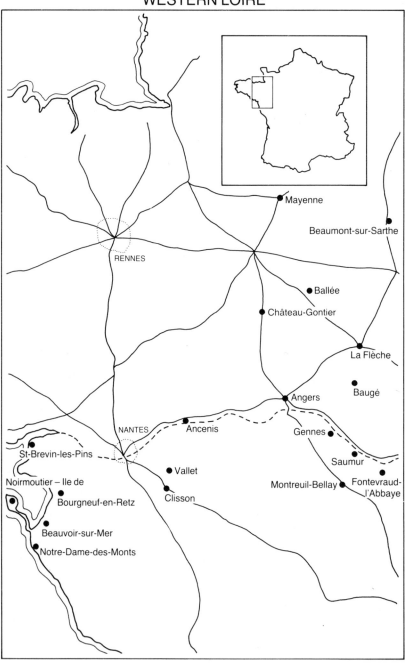

WESTERN LOIRE

The River Loire is best known for its châteaux, those castles and hunting lodges of the French kings, which lie in the so-called 'châteaux country' of Touraine, the 'Garden of France' between Angers and Orléans. Many of these châteaux are quite beautiful, but something equally attractive lies further west along the river in what I usually call the 'castle country' of Anjou. I should explain at this point that in France any large house can be a *château*, while a medieval fortress with battlements is more correctly called a *château-fort*. The castles of Anjou are usually of this latter, warlike kind and largely originated in the twelfth century, when Anjou was ruled by the warlike lord, Fulk Nerra.

Unlike many of the present-day provinces of France – Provence, Burgundy or Brittany, for example – the Western Loire has no historical identity. Parts of it have been filched from Brittany, much of it was once Anjou or Maine, though here we do have an historic connection, for these last two were the ancestral lands of the Plantagenet kings of England, who were also Count of Anjou, and had the Abbey-church at Fontevraud as their mausoleum, and Le Mans as their capital. A modern creation, Western Loire comprises five *départements*: Loire-Atlantique, which was once part of Brittany; the Vendée, a coastal region south of the Loire; Maine-et-Loire, based around Angers; in the north-east, Mayenne; and finally the flatlands of the Sarthe. The whole area is quite delightful, rather off the main tourist track and therefore quite unspoiled, a place that aches to be explored, with a varied cuisine and the excellent wine of Muscadet to wash it down. Access is easy from the north, via Cherbourg, St Malo or Roscoff, and a half-day's drive from the Channel coast will put you in the middle of it and on the banks of the Loire.

Once there, perhaps in the city of Nantes, a good tour would first take the traveller across the river into the Vendée and so down the Atlantic coast past the island of Noirmoutier, which is easily reached across a bridge, and then on to St-Jean-de-Monts and the beaches of Les Sables d'Olonne. This is a summer holiday region, a coastline of rocky coves, sandy beaches and small resorts. Inland, on the way back north to the river, a good route would run through La Roche-sur-Yonne and Clisson, and back to the Loire through the Muscadet country at Ancenis. Turning east, the road along the south bank of the river offers views to the north shore, all the way to Angers, capital of Anjou, a city famous for the manufacture of tapestries. There is a fine castle and a twelfth-century cathedral, plus lots of good hotels and restaurants. South of Angers lies the château of Brissac and the little town of Doue-la-Fontaine, famous for its roses. North of here, across the river, lies the town of Baugé, where a Franco-Scots army thrashed an English force commanded by Thomas, Duke of Clarence in 1421, while further north still, on the banks of the little River Loir lies La Flèche, a very pleasant town just in the Sarthe. When I walked across France in 1987 I remember the Sarthe country as a flat wilderness, with cabbage fields dripping in the rain, but when the sun is out this is beautiful open country, full of orchards, with a litter of brownstone villages to set off the scenery.

Moving east, towards Laval and so into Mayenne – the ancient Maine – good places to visit include Craon, a pleasant town in the valley of the Oudon, with an eighteenth-century white château. South-west of here lies Châteaubriant, which has another, much older château, and from there the Erdre valley runs south back to Nantes and the Loire.

This is a very varied region. It has a long sea-coast, a river estuary and the great Loire itself, plus much farmland, largely given over to pasture, orchards and vineyards. It is a tourist area along the coast, and in parts of the river east of Angers, but in the main this is a purely French region with enough agricultural activity to keep it prosperous without any need to bow to the demands of tourism. A range of fresh local produce means that the cuisine is generally excellent. Finally, to top it off, there are the wines of Muscadet. Those who are looking for somewhere warm, French, and not too far away, should head for the Western Loire.

Essential sights

Angers, for the castle and cathedral. La Baule is a fine seaside resort, though technically in Brittany. Les Rosiers near Gennes is very pretty, and the still-inhabited château at Brissac is well worth

Church of Vincennes, Paris

*Windmills in the Vendée (*photo by kind permission of the French Government Tourist Office*)*

Noyers, Burgundy

A view of Saumur across the Loire

The Great Hérisson waterfall in Franche-Comté

Statue to commemorate the flotteurs of Clamecy in Burgundy

visiting. Still in the Vendée, try Les Sables d'Olonne, and Ile d'Yeu, Noirmoutier and Clisson, or for a typical resort, Pornichet. Other places worth visiting are Châteaubriant, the magnificent town of Nantes, Le Mans, especially outside the time of the 24-hour race, the magnificent castle at Plessis-Macé, and a fine little town, La Roche-sur-Yonne.

Food

The Western Loire cannot boast a distinctly regional cuisine, but there are regional dishes worth looking out for. Instead, it can rightly claim to offer a wide range of appetizing, well-prepared dishes, using fresh produce from the sea, many of them designed to complement the local wine. Eels and trout from the River Loire, mussels, fish and shellfish from the sea, charcuterie and pâtés, mushrooms, and the delicious *Reinette* apple from Maine are just some of the specialities, although to these one can add *rillettes* from Le Mans, potted meat, usually pork or rabbit, *sandre* (pike-perch), and the excellent crab, lobsters and oysters along the Vendée coast and especially in the restaurants of Les Sables d'Olonne, an important fishing port as well as a holiday centre. Look out also for lamb, *pré-salé*, from the salt flats, cheeses such as Caillebot and St Paulin and fish dishes like *coquilles de St-Jacques à la Nantaise*.

Wine

As we shall see, the central Loire is drenched with wine, but although most of it is of the country variety, the widest choice lies in Touraine, further east. Here, in the Western Loire, the principal wine is Muscadet, which comes from the area around Nantes. Muscadet is an excellent complement to fish, oysters, or indeed any seafood. There are three main varieties: Muscadet, which can be rather acid; Muscadet de Sèvre-et-Maine, a dry, light wine with a slightly fruity taste; and Muscadet des Côteaux de la Loire, which tends to be fuller-bodied and rather more tasty. All are AOC. There is also Gros-Plant Muscadet, a light and pleasant wine that comes from the country near Nantes, while Muscadet-sur-Lie is a wine that has rested longer in the pulp, or lees, and is therefore more rounded. All Muscadet can be drunk young. The local reds and a certain amount of rosé come from the Côteaux d'Ancenais on the south bank of the river.

RESTAURANTS

44150 Ancenis

HOTEL LES VOYAGEURS
98 Rue Georges Clemenceau
☎ (40) 83 10 06
Thee are two good *logis* in Ancenis, a quiet little Loire town between Nantes and Angers, but this one serves good local dishes from Brittany and Anjou. Menus from F60 to F125. 16 rooms. Restaurant closed Sunday.

49000 Angers

LE VERT D'EAU
9 Boulevard Gaston-Dumesnil
☎ (41) 48 52 86
A very pleasant town-centre restaurant, once popular with Curnousky ('Le Prince des Gastronomes') and therefore very good, with a notable wine list. Menus from F80 to F195. Best to book for dinner. Closed Sunday and Monday.

53340 Ballée

HOTEL L'HERMITAGE
Saulges
☎ (43) 90 52 28
A good stop *en route* to the Loire from Cherbourg or St Malo, across Mayenne. This 2-star *logis* has 27 rooms, menus from F78 to F180, and very good wines. A worthwhile stop. Restaurant closed Sunday evening and Monday.

49150 Baugé

HOTEL LA BOULE D'OR
4 Rue Cygne
☎ (41) 89 82 12
Baugé is just a little place, but it has history and two *logis*, of which I prefer this one. 11 rooms, menus from F65 to F180, and a warm welcome from M. Jolly. Restaurant closed Sunday evening and Monday.

72170 Beaumont-sur-Sarthe

HOTEL DU CHEMIN DE FER
Near the station
☎ (43) 97 00 05
M. Hary's very agreeable *logis* is by the railway station, a mile or so from Beaumont. He has 16 rooms and a warm welcome to go with the good food in his pleasant dining room. Well worth a stop between Normandy and the Loire, and I stopped here on my walk across France. Menus from F55 to F168. Restaurant closed Sunday evening and Monday lunchtime.

85230 Beauvoir-sur-Mer

HOTEL DU MARCHE
2 Grande Place
☎ (51) 68 71 40
Beauvoir is a fine little seaside resort of the Vendée with two good *logis*. This one has 2 stars and 17 rooms, a restaurant serving local dishes with menus from F65 to F190, and a cheerful staff. Excellent seafood. Very busy during July and August, so book.

44580 Bourgneuf-en-Retz

AUBERGE LA BOURRINE
6–8 Rue de la Taillée
☎ (40) 21 40 69
This little *logis* has only seven rooms but a great reputation for good food – M. Lecoeur won the local *Logis de France* Cookery Contest with his *poisson en beurre blanc*. Menus from F68 to F130.

44250 St-Brevin-les-Pins

HOTEL LA DEBARCADERE
Place de la Marine
☎ (40) 27 20 53
This little resort in Loire-Atlantique, near Pornichet, is a delightful spot to visit, and this hotel, which serves local dishes and excellent seafood, matched by a range of Muscadet, is the best place to stay. 17 rooms and menus from F100 to F130. Very busy in summer, so booking is essential. Restaurant closed Sunday evening outside high season.

53200 Château-Gontier

LE PARC HOTEL ET BRASSERIE
2 et 46 Ave Joffre
☎ (43) 07 28 41
This large 43-room *logis*, with the restaurant-brasserie down the road, deserves its three stars, if only for the cheerful staff. Menus from F85 to F290. Restaurant closed Sunday.

72340 La Châtre-sur-le-Loire

HOTEL DE FRANCE
Town centre
☎ (43) 44 40 16
This is a good hotel of the Sarthe, with an excellent restaurant; one of the gems on the road from Le Mans to Tours. If you come this way, stop the night for M. Pasteau's fine food and the excellent wines of Jasnairès. A popular hotel with drivers in the Le Mans 24-Hour Race, whose pictures line the walls. I stayed here on my walk across France and was made very welcome, as you will be. Not to be missed by *logis* lovers. 28 rooms, menus from F60 to F210.

44190 Clisson

LA BONNE AUBERGE
1 Rue Oliver de Clisson
☎ (40) 54 01 90
This superb restaurant justifies its Michelin rosette with some outstanding dishes and excellent wines. Well worth a detour when exploring the Vendée or heading south. Menus from F72 to F270 – excellent value. Try the *sandre rôti crème langouste* with a Muscadet-sur-Lie wine. Restaurant closed Sunday evening and Monday.

72200 La Flèche

HOTEL LE VERT-GALANT
70 Grande Rue
☎ (43) 94 00 51
La Flèche is a very agreeable riverside town of the Sarthe, well worth lingering in on a summer evening, followed by a night at this cheerful, well-run little hotel. Best to book as there are only 10 rooms. Good menus from F60 to F175, with many local dishes. Restaurant closed Thursday.

49590 Fontevraud-l'Abbaye

HOTEL LA CROIX BLANCHE
Town centre
☎ (41) 51 71 11
This lies just opposite the Plantagenet Abbey and is a very popular *logis*, with comfortable rooms in a new wing and a very good restaurant. The staff are friendly and efficient, and you can park. Thoroughly recommended. 22 rooms, but it is best to book. Menus from F51 to F142.

RESTAURANT LA LICORNE
31 Rue d'Arbrissel
☎ (41) 51 72 49
An elegant little restaurant, tucked away beyond the church at Fontevraud, and best reached through the garden. Excellent food and a good range of Loire wines. Not cheap – our lunch for two cost F520 – but I recall it as being very enjoyable. Well worth a visit and marvellous on a sunny day.

49350 Gennes

AUBERGE JEANNE DE LAVAL
54 Rue Nationale
Les Rosiers-sur-Loire
☎ (41) 51 80 17
An excellent riverside restaurant, famed locally for M. Augereau's superb cooking. Menus from F170 to F300, not cheap but first-class and good value. The cellar has a vast selection of local wines and the service is superb.

HOSTELLERIE DE LA LOIRE
9 Rue des Cadets de Saumur
☎ (41) 51 81 03
An agreeable *logis* by the Loire, with 11 rooms and menus from F55 to F135, serving good local dishes. Try the trout with almonds, new potatoes and a bottle of chilled Muscadet. Restaurant closed Monday evening and Tuesday.

LE PRIEURE
Town centre
☎ (41) 67 90 14
You will have to book to dine at Le Prieuré, so ask for directions when doing so. It stands in a park overlooking the Loire between Saumur and Gennes, and is a 4-star hotel with 30 rooms and this excellent Michelin rosette restaurant. Try the *lotte aux palourdes*. Excellent

wines, many from local vineyards. Not cheap – expect to pay F300 per head – but probably worth it.

72600 Mamers

HOTEL AU BON LABOUREUR
1 Rue Paul Bert
☎ (43) 97 60 27
A quiet little *logis* deep in the Sarthe, an ideal base for exploring this lovely, unassuming part of France between Normandy and the Loire. 10 rooms, menus from F70 to F150. Restaurant closed Friday evening and Saturday.

53100 Mayenne

LA CROIX COUVERTE
Route d'Alençon
☎ (43) 04 32 48
This terraced country-house restaurant with 13 rooms lies outside the town on the road for Alençon and Normandy. Good traditional cooking, well presented, with excellent wines. Menus at F78 and F128. Worth a stop. Restaurant closed Sunday evening from October to May.

49260 Montreuil-Bellay

SPLENDID'HOTEL (ET RELAIS DU BELLAY)
Town centre
☎ (41) 52 30 21
You must dine at the *relais* since the hotel has no restaurant, but the combination is attractive. The hotel has 40 pleasant rooms, the *relais* several good menus from F65 to F200, and pleasant staff and good wines. Can get crowded at weekends. Restaurant closed Sunday evening from September to Easter.

85330 Noirmoutier (Ile de)

HOTEL FLEUR DE SEL
Near the church
Rue des Saulniers
☎ (51) 39 21 59
Noirmoutier is an island off the Vendée coast, reached by a bridge or a causeway. This 2-star *logis* has 35 rooms and good food, especially seafood and shellfish, with menus from F120 to F180. Try the local *moules*, which are superb in a cream sauce. Best to book well ahead for July/August.

RESTAURANT ST-PAUL
Bois de la Chaise
☎ (51) 39 05 63
Great plates of *fruits de mer*, clams, shrimps, *langoustines*, fine fresh fish from the harbour, good chilled wines, excellent cheese-board. You will lunch or dine well at no great cost. Menus from F120 to F170 – or an extensive *à la carte*. Rooms available.

85690 Notre-dame-des-Monts

HOTEL DU CENTRE
Place de l'Eglise
☎ (51) 58 83 05
M. Brunet won the Vendée round of the *Logis de France* Cookery Competition in 1987, and has kept his standards high. 17 rooms and good food in a beamed restaurant, close to the beach, make this hotel well worth a detour. Try the 'Menu Gastro' – poached turbot, *magret de canard*, six excellent courses for F155. Other menus from F50 to F180.

49400 Saumur

LES MENESTRELS
11 Rue Raspail
☎ (41) 67 71 10
Saumur is not over-blessed with good restaurants, which is surprising in such an attractive town, but you will eat well here. Menus from F103 to F190, and a good selection of Loire wines. Closed Sunday evening and Monday except during July and August.

44330 Vallet

AUBERGE DE LA GARE
44 Rue St Vincent
☎ (40) 33 92 55
This little *auberge* is near Clisson and the Muscadet country, in a quiet little village. 15 rooms and menus from F55 to F150. Nice people who welcome any visitor. Restaurant closed Sunday.

VAL DE LOIRE

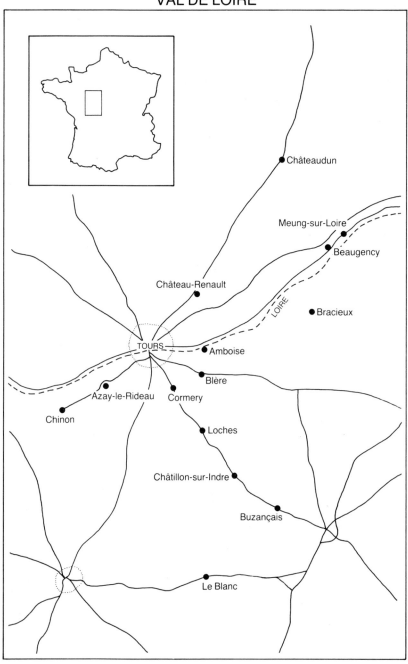

VAL DE LOIRE

The Val de Loire, Loire Valley, or Central Loire region, call it what you will, occupies a large area of central France, straddling the heart of that famous French river. The Loire actually rises in the remote Ardèche, on the slopes of the Gerbier de Jonc, and flows for 600 miles before it reaches the sea near Nantes, but no part of that journey is more beautiful or more historic than that through the 'châteaux country' of Touraine.

Like the Western Loire, the Val de Loire is a modern creation, although enfolding a number of ancient counties and dukedoms within its present boundaries. These boundaries embrace six *départements*, which are, from the West, Indre-et-Loire, which with Indre further south and Cher to the east covers much of the old Dukedom of Berri; to the north lies Eure-et-Loir; Loir-et-Cher; and finally in the north-east corner, Loiret. The River Loire makes a great bow across this region, reaching its most northern point at Orléans – capital of another dukedom – before sliding south and west towards the sea.

Few areas in France are so varied or so rewarding as this 'châteaux country'. It has good weather, beautiful countryside and attractive, prosperous towns, some of considerable size. It also contains those fabled 'châteaux of the Loire', though be aware that many of those 'Loire' chateaux actually lie on other rivers, the Cher, Vienne or Indre, each a tributary of the main river but possessing attractive valleys of its own. The region between, say, Saumur and Orléans, is full of tourists from May to September, when even the smaller roads have too much coach traffic, so if possible visit it in April/May or October, when the countryside is as beautiful and the crowds much smaller.

Apart from the châteaux, the great attraction of this area is the towns, many of which are worth visiting. Saumur has a splendid castle, a *château-fort*, and the famous Cadre Noir, the French cavalry display team. Orléans and Tours are bustling cities. Blois has splendid buildings on the river. Chinon, though small, is *magnifique*, the home of Rabelais, full of memorials to Joan of Arc, and crowned by a splendid, if ruined, castle. Bourges, the capital of Berri has the finest cathedral in France outside Chartres. And if all this is not enough, there are the smaller places such as Beaugency, Châteaudun, Loches, Argentan-sur-Creuse, Fontevraud, Amboise, Montsoreau, and many others worth visiting.

I have cycled and walked extensively through this region over the years and still not run out of fresh places to visit. I can only encourage people to go there and tour on the minor roads, stopping and starting as the fancy takes them.

Essential sights

The châteaux are the pegs on which any visit to the region should be hung, but there are so many in this area that it pays to be selective. The Green Michelin *Châteaux of the Loire* is the best guide to the châteaux and all they contain, but some are so outstanding that they really deserve special mention. They all owe their existence to one of two factors. The first is that this Loire country was a march between the Counts of Anjou and Touraine, who began most of the fortresses and built the early castles. Later on, these were extended or rebuilt during the Hundred Years War. Secondly, the great forests of the region were the favourite hunting grounds of the French kings from the time of Charles VII until the reign of Louis XIII, and they built many of the most striking châteaux, often, as at Azay-le-Rideau, on the site of an old *château-fort*.

My personal choice would be as follows. *Châteaux-forts*: Chinon, Angers, Loches, Saumur, Amboise, Beaugency. Châteaux: Chenonceaux, Chambord, Azay-le-Rideau, Valençay, Villandry – this last because it has beautiful gardens with 30 miles of low box hedges and a thousand lime trees set among the flower-beds. If any chateau offers a *son-et-lumière* show, try and see it.

Food

The area can claim many notable dishes, such as *quenelles de brochet*, made with Loire pike. The food in Berri tends to be solid country fare, of the kind often found in provincial areas. Try the soups or the *poulet en Barbouille*. The region has absorbed the best dishes from all the other areas of France and improved them with skill, care and fresh local produce. The discerning traveller will eat very well along the Loire, but local dishes to look out for will include the *tarte-tatin*, the delicious upside-down apple cake from the Orléannais, and a wide range of excellent cheeses, such as St Maure, Chabichou or Livroux, this last with a distinctive pyramid shape, or my personal favourite, Crottin de Chavignol. Goat's cheese is sometimes served hot, as a first course *en croute* – 'goat on toast', as my friends have come to call it. Touraine, the Garden of France, naturally produces excellent fruit and vegetables, so the strawberries, grapes, apples and peaches are first-class. Many Loire fish dishes come with *beurre blanc*, a sauce of shallots, wine and butter. There is also an abundance of game from the forests, so venison and wild boar are often found on offer in the *à la carte*. Pâtés are a speciality of Touraine.

Wine

There is so much wine in this area that it is hard to know where to start, but let us begin by saying that the Loire wines are very good, come in every colour, and are generally reasonably priced. With nearly 800 square miles of vineyards, they are also abundant. It is said that the Loire wines cannot stand comparison with the wines of Bordeaux or Burgundy, which may well be so, but some are nevertheless excellent, with a sound history and solid appeal. Certainly, when I am in the Loire, I stick rigidly to the local wines, and even after over 20 years of visits I am never stuck for choice.

For a white wine that deserves to be better known, try Jasnairès, which comes from a small area around Le Châtre-sur-le-Loir. For good reds, try those of Chinon, Bourgueil and St-Nicolas-de-Bourgueil and Montlouis take some beating, while for more good whites there is Vouvray, Sancerre and Azay-le-Rideau and the fruity Pouilly-Fumé from Pouilly-sur-Loire. A good sparkling white comes from Saumur. I also like and therefore recommend the rosés from Anjou or Touraine; Rosé d'Anjou is popular all over France. The Val de Loire is a land of wine and I recommend you to try them while you are there and turn your back on wines from other regions – at least during your stay.

RESTAURANTS

37400 Amboise

L'AUBERGE DU MAIL
32 Quai Général de Gaulle
☎ (47) 57 60 39
This agreeable *logis* on the banks of the Loire is one of four in Amboise, a great number for such a small town. 12 rooms, menus from F75 to F160, good local wines on an extensive list. Restaurant closed Friday outside July and August.

LE MANOIR ST THOMAS
Place Richelieu
☎ (47) 57 22 52
This quiet little restaurant is the place to dine in Amboise, thanks to François Le Coz's excellent cooking. Try the *rosette d'agneau à la grace de porto*, if you don't believe me. Menus from F200 to F250 – not cheap, but well worth it. Closed Monday.

37190 Azay-le-Rideau

L'AUTOMATE GOURMAND
1 Rue du Parc
La Chapelle-St-Blaise
☎ (47) 45 39 07
This little restaurant lies just across the river from Azay, and is a real find. The curious name comes from the fact that half the restaurant is occupied by mechanical toys, but the service is good, the menus (from F75) excellent value, and there is an extensive wine list. The restaurant is quite small, so get there early, and book if possible. Closed Wednesday and Sunday evening.

HOTEL DU GRAND MONARQUE
Place de la République
☎ (47) 45 40 08
Serge Jacquet runs the hotel and Alain Brisacier does the cooking, and the combination makes this a fabled *logis* of the Loire. 28 rooms, and dishes like *poissons de Loire au beurre blanc*. Menus from F135 to F250. As a bonus, the château of Azay is only yards away.

45190 Beaugency

HOSTELLERIE DE L'ECU DE BRETAGNE
Place du Martroi
☎ (38) 44 67 60

I have stayed in this *hostellerie* several times over the years and have always enjoyed the food and the welcome. It also has secluded parking. M. Conan runs a very fine and very popular hotel, with 26 rooms and menus from F80 to F150, as well as some notable Loire wines.

HOTEL DE LA SOLOGNE
Place St Firmin
☎ (38) 44 50 27
This hotel is set in a quiet square near the statue of Joan of Arc, below the castle keep. As you enter it appears to be filled with plants and flowers. 16 comfortable rooms, a pleasant panelled bar and dining room – a good place to stay. Menus from F70.

36300 Le Blanc

HOTEL L'ILE D'AVANT
Route de Chateauroux
☎ (54) 37 01 56
I can't think why more people don't visit Le Blanc to go walking or birdwatching in the lake country of the Brenne; quite delightful. Those who do should stay in this 2-star *logis*, with menus from F50 to F200 and 15 comfortable rooms. Restaurant closed Sunday evening and Monday.

37156 Blère

HOTEL LE CHEVAL-BLANC
Place de l'Eglise
☎ (47) 30 30 14
A lady wrote to me once, saying she loved France and French food, but couldn't stand the French. Well, it takes all sorts, I thought, but I sent her to this charming hotel in Blère, where Michel and Micheline Blériot make a point of welcoming their guests and have even won awards for their hospitality. This is the perfect hotel, with 13 rooms (so be sure to book) and excellent food on all the menus from F85 to F200. Excellent wine list. Well worth a detour.

HOTEL DU CHER
9 Rue du Pont
☎ (47) 57 95 15
A small 1-star hotel, just down the road from Le Cheval-Blanc, and somewhat cheaper, with menus from F63 to F145. An excellent *hors d'oeuvre* chariot . . . with quails' eggs. A good wine list.

LE CLAIR-COTTAGE HOTEL
Rue de l'Europe
Chenonceaux-Chisseaux
☎ (47) 23 90 69
This pleasant little hotel is actually several miles outside Blère, near the château of Chenonceaux. It is a rambling, friendly place, with lots of parking and the ever-helpful Mme Bourbonnais. Not expensive, with menus from F58 to F120. 21 rooms.

41250 Bracieux

HOTEL DU GRAND ST MICHEL
Face en Château
Chambord
☎ (54) 20 31 31
This attractive hotel-restaurant is directly opposite Chambord, which, with Chenonceaux, is one of the two Loire châteaux that no one should miss. Try the excellent F90 menu and stay in one of the 38 bedrooms. Other menus from F100 to F200. This is an elegant *logis* with large rooms and a sunny terrace. Well worth a visit.

36500 Buzançais

HOTEL DU CROISSANT
53 Rue Grande
☎ (54) 84 00 49
This is a little hotel with a great heart and the most friendly management, right in the centre of this town on the Indre. 10 rooms and menus from F80 to F180 – excellent value. Restaurant closed Friday evening.

28200 Châteaudun

L'ARNAUDIERE
Auberge du Château
4 Rue St Lubin
☎ (37) 45 98 98
We had the best bottle of St Nicolas de Bourgeuil I have ever tasted in this cheerful, elegant restaurant near the castle, where M. and Mme Patrick Thuillery serve excellent local dishes to match the local wines. Menus from F95. Closed Monday.

HOTEL DE LA ROSE
12 Rue Lambert-Licors
☎ (37) 45 21 83

A small, friendly *logis* with seven rooms and good food on menus from F90 to F200. Restaurant closed Sunday evening.

Château-Renault

HOTEL LION D'OR
166 Rue de la République
☎ (47) 29 66 50
This little 10-room hotel has a superb and elegant restaurant, where chef Christian Guignard offers menus from F70 to F170, with dishes like *Filet de boeuf des Gastronomes* and *Bouilletine d'anguille au Chinon*. Excellent value, well worth a stop.

36700 Châtillon-sur-Indre

AUBERGE DE LA TOUR
2 Route du blanc
☎ (54) 38 72 17
The family Nicolas, who run this friendly family hotel, made me very welcome on my walk through France, and will do as much for you. 10 rooms, and good food on menus from F65 to F180. Restaurant closed Sunday evening and Monday. Worth a stop.

37500 Chinon

GRAND-HOTEL DE LA BOULE D'OR
66 Quai Jeanne d'Arc
☎ (47) 93 03 13
In spite of the imposing name, this cheerful 2-star *logis* is a friendly place beside the Loire, just below the castle where St Joan first met the Dauphin. 20 rooms, good – often very good – dishes with menus from F70 to F200, but I remember the welcome best. May be crowded in summer, so it is best to book. Restaurant closed Sunday evening and Monday.

37320 Cormery

L'AUBERGE DU MAIL
Place du Mail
☎ (47) 43 40 32
You may have a little trouble finding Cormery – on the Indre south of Tours – and even more trouble finding L'Auberge du Mail, but this restaurant serves some of the best food in this part of France, and the young Girandons are a delightful couple. Jean-Jacques' cooking pulls in the crowds, so book if possible, and expect to pay about F150 for lunch or dinner. There are also three bedrooms, one of which I stayed

in on my walk across France, reading a vast supply of Astérix books. Definitely not one to miss, but very small, so book if possible.

37600 Loches

LUCCOTEL
Rue des Lézards
☎ (47) 91 50 50
The Luccotel lies outside Loches, on a small plateau, and is a modern hotel with 42 big, bright rooms and an elegant dining room that looks out over Loches to the great white keep of the castle. The service is impeccable and I had a superb meal with *saumon et barbue marines au citron et au poivre vert*, with half a bottle of Vouvray and a selection of local cheeses from St Maur and Valençay. I rate this hotel and restaurant highly and other friends who have tried it also found it excellent. Menus from F65 to F160.

45130 Meung-sur-Loire

LE RABELAIS
Near the church
☎ (38) 45 11 55
We came by this restaurant one Sunday lunchtime, and by 12.45 it was crammed. Fortunately, it operates on two floors, but go here for the stupendous buffet, the cheerful staff, the excellent fresh food and the wines of Chinon, which our waitress insisted on serving *un peu frais*, and quite right too. Menus from F75 to F175. Good wines – a real experience.

BURGUNDY

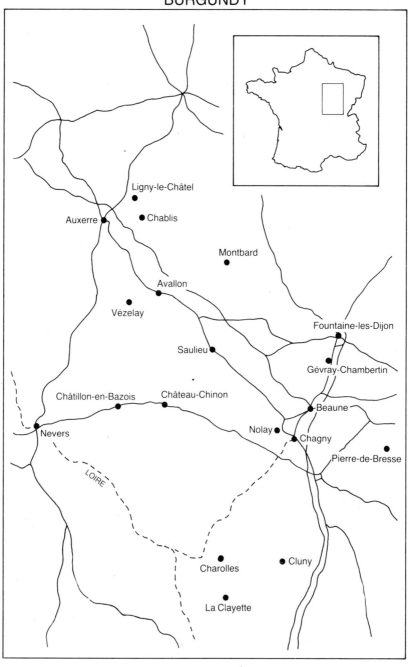

BURGUNDY

Burgundy presents the writer with a paradox, for it is not only one of the great gastronomic areas of France, famous for both food and wine, but is also an area which the foreign visitor has largely overlooked. This is a surprise and a pity, for few areas of France have as much to offer the visitor, not least a rare combination of good weather, spectacular scenery, marvellous history and excellent wine. I think this neglect stems from the fact that Burgundy, lying in central France, is both too far and too near, a place just out of reach, or a place of passage on the road south. But those who stop on the way through the region are in for a delightful surprise.

History begins early in Burgundy, for it was here, near Alise-Ste-Reine that Julius Caesar beat the Gallic chieftain Vercingetorix, and so completed his conquest of Gaul. Burgundy later became a great fief of the Kingdom of France, reaching the peak of its power between 1364 and 1477, when it was ruled by the four great Valois Dukes of Burgundy: Philip the Bold, John the Fearless, Philip the Good and Charles the Rash, who ruled half of Western Europe from their capitals in Dijon and Brussels. Whole books have been written about Burgundy and the Dukes – I've written a couple myself – but in spite of such efforts, the area remains largely unknown. Those who like to avoid the madding crowd can do so here with ease, while enjoying the most excellent food and wine.

Modern Burgundy is much smaller than the old Dukedom, but it is still a long province, transfixed by the N7 and the Paris–Lyon–Marseille autoroute, both of which should be abandoned for smaller D-class roads. Bounded on the west by the Loire, the present province includes the *départements* of Yonne, Nièvre (the Nivernais), Côte d'Or and Saône-et-Loire. Within this area there is a great deal to see and enjoy, so a good guidebook is essential, but among places I can personally recommend are the wine towns of Beaune and Chablis, the cities of Nevers, Dijon, Mâcon and Auxerre, little places such as Nolay, which is a real medieval town, quite rare; Vézelay, a famous pilgrim town and one of the starting points on the Road to Compostela; Saulieu, which has several good restaurants; Semur-en-Auxois, which has mighty walls, as does Flavigny, Autun and Sens, which have fine cathedrals, and the little villages along the Canal du Nivernais, up to Clamecy. Burgundy is a place to rove about in by car or bike or canal barge, but if you mark the following places on your map and link them up on minor roads, I feel sure you will see enough to bring you back again.

Essential sights

Beaune, to see the Hôtel-Dieu, the fifteenth-century hospital. Dijon, Vézelay, for the pilgrim church. The Lac des Settons in the Morvan Park, the Canal de Bourgogne or the Canal du Nivernais, ideal for a cruising holiday. Auxerre, Sens and Autun, for their fine cathedrals. Nolay, a gem, as is Noyers, on the River Serein. Nevers on the Loire. The abbeys at Pontigny and Fontenay. The châteaux at Ratilly in the Nièvre, and Tanlay on the River Armaçon. Tournous on the Saône. Châtillon-sur-Seine, to see the marvellous golden treasure of Vix, a wonderful collection of Celtic jewellery.

Food

As befits a rich province, Burgundy is a gastronomic centre, drawing on produce from its own fields and the regions round about, creating food to match the wine. The traditional element in food cooked *à la bourguignonne* is wine, of which *boeuf bourguignonne* or *coq au vin* are the most famous examples. Snails – *escargots* – are another Burgundian speciality, as are *quenelles de brochet* from the Saône. *Jambon persille*, ham pressed with parsley, *marcassin*, young wild boar, *pain d'épices*, gingerbread from Dijon and mustard from the same area, cheese from the Charollais, with Citeaux, Epoise, St Florentin and Chaource as other examples. The great Morvan forest, which divides the Côte d'Or from the Nivernais, is another gastronomic region, specializing in more country fare, such as *potée bourguignonne*, a vegetable soup, or the delicious *rapée morvandelle*, grated potato mixed with cheese and eggs. The beef from the Charolais is excellent, as are cheeses from the Yonne and ham from the Morvan.

A great fish dish is *pochouse*, a casserole of freshwater fish from the Saône.

Wine

Burgundian wines will repay a lifetime's study. Wine drinkers are broadly divided into those who like Burgundy and those who will drink anything. I belong to the latter school, but if I had to choose, it would be Burgundy. Some of the Burgundy wines are famous vintages and therefore very expensive. Montrachet, Romanée-Conti, and many of the better-known vintage command breathtaking prices, but are probably worth every centime. More ordinary folk will find a great deal of drinkable wine at moderate cost. For white wine lovers may I recommend the wines of Pouilly-Fuissé or Mâcon, or some of the Chablis, or a good Côte de Beaune. The Côte d'Or is one long escarpment, divided by the town of Beaune into the Côte de Beaune in the south (Beaune, Pommard, Volnay, Meursault, Montrachet, etc), and the Côte de Nuits (Gévray-Chambertain, Clos-Vougeot, Romanée-Conti, Nuits-St-Georges, etc) to the north. Most of the Côte de Nuits wines are reds. The great aperitif here is *Kir*, dry white wine with a dash of *cassis*.

When people ask me to recommend a region of France which 'has the lot and not too many tourists' – a demand which is a contradiction in terms – I usually suggest Burgundy. No one has ever thought of going there, and no one who goes there is ever disappointed, but if you are a 'serious' wine lover, then I recommend close study of an up-to-date wine primer before you leave for the wine-drenched villages of Burgundy.

RESTAURANTS

89000 Auxerre

HOTEL DE SEIGNELAY
2 Rue du Pont
☎ (86) 52 03 48
Auxerre is a very fine provincial town, a port on the Canal du Nivernais, and must be visited. This excellent hotel, a rather large *logis*, has 23 rooms and adequate menus from F59 to F160. A good wine list.

89200 Avallon

HOTEL LES CAPUCINS
6 Ave Paul Doumer
☎ (86) 34 06 52
Avallon, the birthplace of Vauban, Louis XIV's military architect, is a nice little town, a good touring centre close to Vézelay. This hotel serves good local dishes on menus from F110 to F270. Only eight rooms, so it is best to book. Restaurant closed Tuesday evening and Wednesday outside high season.

21200 Beaune

HOTEL CENTRAL
2 Rue Victor Millot
☎ (80) 24 77 24
This is where I usually stay when visiting Beaune, a 3-star *logis* with 20 inexpensive rooms and a notably good restaurant. Menus from F71 to F230. A good range of Burgundian wines in an extensive wine list.

HOTEL DE LA CLOCHE
40–42 Rue de Faubourg-Madeleine
☎ (80) 24 66 33
Beaune has a number of good *logis*, but the Cloche serves good Burgundian food, has 15 rooms and menus from F80 to F180. Restaurant closed Monday evening and Tuesday.

89800 Chablis

HOSTELLERIE DE CLOS
Rue Jules Rathier
☎ (86) 42 10 63
This little town is a wine centre, so choose local dishes to go with the local vintages, both of which can be found at this excellent hotel. 26 rooms and menus from F132 to F325. Restaurant closed Wednesday, outside high season. The great attraction of this hotel is Michel Vignaud's excellent cooking, but the hotel itself is very comfortable and the town delightful, set in the heart of the Chablis vineyards.

71150 Chagny

HOTEL BONNARD
Route N6 for Chalon
☎ (85) 87 21 49
Most people come to Chagny to eat at Lameloise in the Place d'Annes, which has no less than three Michelin rosettes. Do so by all means,

but recoup a little cash by staying at the Bonnard which has 20 rooms and perfectly adequate menus priced from F65 to F150.

71120 Charolles

HOTEL MODERNE
Ave de la Gare
☎ (85) 24 07 02
I stumbled on the Hôtel Moderne some years ago, and now rarely miss it when passing through Burgundy. Very pleasant staff and excellent food. 18 rooms. Menus from F90 to F220. Highly recommended. Restaurant closed Sunday evening and Monday outside July and August.

58120 Château-Chinon

HOTEL AU VIEUX MORVAN
8 Place Gudin
☎ (86) 85 05 01
The Morvan Park is one of the glories of Burgundy, and this little town of the Nivernais is an excellent touring centre. The hotel serves local dishes, including *sanglier* (wild boar) from the woods. 23 rooms and menus from F70 to F150.

58110 Châtillon-en-Bazois

HOTEL DE LA POSTE
Town centre
☎ (86) 84 14 68
Châtillon is a delightful little town, well worth a visit on any tour of the Nivernais. This hotel has 12 rooms, and good menus, with local dishes, ranging from F50 to F130. Restaurant closed Sunday evening and Monday outside high season.

71800 La Clayette

HOTEL DE LA GARE
38 Ave de la Gare
☎ (85) 28 01 65
A small 2-star *logis* with 9 rooms in the town centre and at no great distance from the castle. Menus from F60 to F200 and very good food. Restaurant closed Sunday evening and Monday outside July and August.

HOTEL DE LA POSTE ET DU DAUPHIN
17 Rue Central
☎ (85) 28 02 45

Good pâtés, excellent fish and Charollais beef are just some of the excellent dishes on offer here, where menus are priced from F60 to F170. A good country hotel and restaurant in a pleasant town. 15 rooms. Recommended.

71250 Cluny

HOTEL MODERNE
Pont de l'Etang
☎ (85) 59 05 65

A cheerful little *logis*, this is the perfect place to stay while visiting Cluny. Although the great abbey was destroyed during the Revolution, much remains of the nice little town. The Moderne has a very good cellar and excellent food. 15 rooms. Menus from F100 to F200. Highly recommended.

21121 Fontaine-les-Dijon

CASTEL BURGUND
3 Route de Troyes
Daix
☎ (80) 56 59 72

Dijon has many hotels but this 2-star *logis* lies outside the town at Fontaine, where Mme Barthelet offers a warm welcome to all visitors. There are 38 rooms, useful when the hotels in Dijon are full.

21220 Gévray-Chambertin

LES MILLESIMES
25 Rue d'Eglise
☎ (80) 51 84 24

One great restaurant among several hereabouts, Les Millésimes is a one-Michelin rosette establishment with menus from F175 to F400 for the meal of a lifetime. Excellent range of Burgundian wines but the house wines are always good and quite reasonable. Closed Tuesday.

89144 Ligny-le-Châtel

AUBERGE DU BIEF
2 Ave de Chablis
☎ (86) 47 43 42

A highly recommended little restaurant in the country north-east of

Auxerre. Good menus ranging widely from F98 to F250. I recommend the *rognons de veau au poivre,* or local fish with a good Chablis. Closed Monday evening and Tuesday.

RELAIS ST VINCENT
14 Grande Rue
☎ (86) 47 53 38
A very pleasant town-centre *logis,* well run by Mme Cointre. 10 rooms and a pleasant restaurant with menus from F70 to F120, all containing a selection of local dishes.

21500 Montbard

HOTEL DE L'ECU
7 Rue Auguste Carre
☎ (80) 92 11 66
A good hotel-restaurant in this fine town of the Côte d'Or, with 25 rooms and well-assorted menus priced from F85 to F260. Recommended.

5800 Nevers

HOTEL LA FOLIE
Route des Saulaies
☎ (86) 57 05 31
I regard Nevers as a Loire town, but it lies in the Nivernais, which is part of Burgundy, so it must be mentioned here. A pretty little town, famous for *faïence* pottery and for the relics of Saint Bernadette. This is a town well worth visiting. La Folie lies 2½ miles out of town on the D504, and has 27 rooms and menus from F55 to F155, offering local dishes.

21340 Nolay

HOTEL DE CHEVREUIL
Town centre
☎ (80) 21 71 89
Nolay is a beautiful little town, with narrow medieval streets – quite delightful. This central hotel has 14 rooms, and serves local dishes in the pleasant dining room. Menus from F61 to F170. Recommended. Restaurant closed Wednesday outside high season.

HOTEL STE-MARIE
Town centre
☎ (80) 21 73 19
Patrice Fechoz won the Burgundy finals of the *Logis de France*

Cookery Contest with his *oeufs en meurette*. This is also a good centre for exploring the Côte d'Or and the vineyards, and like the Chevreuil this little 1-star *logis* with 12 rooms also serves local dishes. Menus from F70 to F145. Restaurant closed Wednesday outside high season.

71270 Pierre-de-Bresse

HOTEL DOUBS-RIVAGE
Charette
☎ (85) 76 23 45
Charette is a little place south-east of Beaune on the D73, where this small 10-room *logis* is the only place to stay. The restaurant serves local dishes with menus from F65 to F160 – excellent value. Recommended. Restaurant closed Sunday evening and Monday outside high season.

21210 Saulieu

HOTEL DE BOURGOGNE
9 Rue Courtepée
☎ (80) 64 08 41
Saulieu is a famous little town on the main N7 road full of good hotels, including this 2-star *logis*, which serves food with local dishes on several inexpensive menus from F60 to F200. 16 rooms.

89450 Vézelay

LE RELAIS DU MORVAN
Village centre
☎ (86) 33 25 33
No visitor to Burgundy can afford to miss the pilgrim town of Vézelay, a starting point on the Road to Compostela. This little *relais* serves local dishes and has inexpensive menus from F75 to F150. Only 9 rooms, so it is best to book ahead, and essential to do so from June to September. Restaurant closed Tuesday and Wednesday outside high season.

JURA – FRANCHE-COMTE

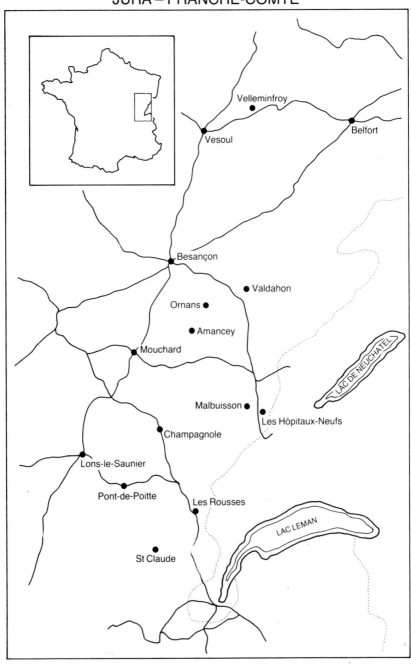

JURA
FRANCHE-COMTE

The Franche-Comté is one of those half-hidden corners of France into which foreign visitors rarely venture. This is a great pity, because the most noticeable physical aspect of the region, the hills of the Jura – hills which gave the word Jurassic to geology – are quite beautiful. Franche-Comté is a paradise for country lovers, in both summer and winter, full of attractive villages and small country towns. Imagine a Gallic Cotswolds and you will have an idea of the Jura and the surrounding country.

Natural beauty apart, there is history. The Franche-Comté was that part of the medieval Duchy of Burgundy which owed homage not to the King of France but to the Holy Roman Emperor. It did not become part of France until 1678, when Louis XIV finally ousted the Hapsburgs and had his title ratified by the Treaty of Nijmegen. This done, Louis proceeded to fortify this latest frontier and sent his great military architect, Vauban, to oversee the works. As a result, Franche-Comté is studded with mighty towns-of-war and great castles, with the ramparts of Besançon being among the finest examples of seventeenth-eighteenth-century fortifications.

The modern Franche-Comté, which now consists of three *départements*, Haute-Saône, Doubs and Jura, is best regarded as a holiday region. In the winter the hills are popular with cross-country skiers, and the *Grande Traversée de la Jura*, a 100-mile trail which runs right across the spine of the Doubs and Jura, is the ultimate challenge for cross-country ski tourers. In summer this famous challenge is the GR5 footpath of the *Grande Randonnée.*

To tour this region properly, some time must be spent on foot – or skis – for this is above all an outdoor area, full of streams and lakes and rushing rivers, perfect for fishermen, walkers and birdwatchers. Access is easy – a long day's drive south-eastwards from Paris, delivers travellers into the Haute-Saône, while the whole Jura Massif, which straddles the Franco-Swiss frontier, is easily reached from the airport at Geneva.

Coming in from the west, most travellers will head for Besançon, the capital of the region, perhaps via Vesoul in the centre of the Haute-Saône, the ideal centre for the northern part of the Jura Massif, and close to the Territoire de Belfort, a little enclave famous for the fact that it never surrendered to the Prussian armies in 1870. Besançon looks like a capital city, crowned today by the Vauban citadel. This fortress contains a marvellous, if tragic, museum commemorating the local Resistance activity during the Second World War. Other sights not to be missed in Besançon include the Grande Rue, parts of which date back to Roman times, and the Musée des Beaux Arts, which contains works by Fragonard and Courbet, the local painter, who came from Ornans. The most famous local son was Victor Hugo, who was born in Besançon, at 140 Grande Rue, in 1802.

From Besançon head north-east to Baume-les-Dames, a pretty town in the valley of the Doubs. North-east again from here, you come to Montbéliard, the home of Peugeot cars, but which is still dominated by a fine fifteenth-century castle. Turn south here, skirting the Jura, to little Montbenoît, starting point for the *Grande Traverseé de la Jura* or the GR5 footpath. Montbenoît is the capital of the Saugeais, a remote valley set off by the fifteenth-sixteenth-century Abbey of St Claude. From here, follow the Jura Massif south to Pontarlier and Salins-les-Bains, to see the Château de Joux, once a prison, and the thermal springs of the spa at Salins. Turn off at Champagnole to see the great waterfall at Hérisson, a great bridal veil of water pouring down a sheer rock face. From now on you are in the Jura proper and should revel in splendid scenery, notably at Baume-les-Messieurs, which is notable for the void of the Cirque de Baume, where the sheer rock walls of three ravines combine into a breathtaking sight. The most southern point on this journey is the town of St Claude, which has another great waterfall, aptly called the Queue de Cheval, the Horse's Tail. This town is famous for the manufacture of pipes.

Heading north again, pleasant sights continue. Lons-le-Saunier was the birthplace of Rouget de Lisle, who composed a march – *Le Chant de Guerre de l'Armée du Rhin*, better known today as La Marseillaise. Lons is the capital of the Jura *département*, and I recommend a visit to the town museum to see more works by Courbet before driving down the river to visit Ornans, a very pretty village – or, since it has a charter dating from 1244, really a town. Courbet was born here in 1819, and his home can be visited. East of here lies Dôle, once the capital of the entire Franche-Comté, and much of the medieval town still remains, scattered along the banks of the Doubs. Dôle is famous as the birthplace of Louis Pasteur, another famous son of the Franche-Comté, who was born here in 1822.

Franche-Comté, with the crowning glory of the Jura, is a delightful, little-known part of France, full of pretty places, fresh, green and virtually unexplored by the foreign visitor. Put it on your list of places to visit, but go there soon, before the word leaks out.

Essential sights

The Jura hills and the great Hérisson waterfall. The citadel in Besançon. The works of Courbet at Ornans. The Cirque de Baume. The wine centre at Arbois.

Food

As one might expect in a country region, most of the local food is simple fare, improved by fresh ingredients. Cheese fondues are popular, and Comté cheese, full of holes like Gruyère, is probably the most famous product. The ham is excellent, and one regional speciality is *bresi*, cured beef served in thin strips. There is game in the woods, so venison and wild boar appear in casseroles and pâtés, and the many lakes and rivers produce excellent trout, and pike for *quenelles de brochet*. Local dishes to look out for on the menus include *croustade Jurassien*, a cheese and bacon pastry. Anything described as *Jurassien* or *Comtoise* comes with cheese and ham, like *escalope de veau Comtoise*, which is veal in breadcrumbs, cooked with cheese and ham strips. Look out too for *pochuse* or *meurette*, a casserole of freshwater fish, found widely in the Jura to Rhône region, and the *poulet au vin jaune*, chicken with mushrooms in a wine and cream sauce. There are a great many Jura cheeses, which apart from Comté, include Chevret, which is a soft goat's cheese, and among the cow's-milk cheeses, Mamirolle, Emmental and the Bleu de Gex.

Wine

The local wine is rather good, with the wines of Arbois ranked AC. The local *vin jaune*, the *vin de paille* or straw-wine, are unusual wines, rather like sherry and not to my personal taste, but the Arbois dry rosé is the most distinguished. The wines of the Côtes du Jura come in all colours and kinds, red, rosé, white, *gris-de-gris* and bubbly. Although only the Jura produces wine today, many wine lists contain the excellent vins de pays du Franche-Comté, again in red, white or rosé, light and dry, a change from the rather overwhelming *vin jaune*. If you can find it, the white wine from L'Etoile is very good. There is also a range of locally brewed spirits, some of them eye-watering, and the Hypocras, a kind of punch, of red wine and spices, which is really best avoided.

RESTAURANTS

25330 Amancey

HOTEL DE LA POSTE
Nans-sous-Ste-Anne
☎ (81) 86 62 57
A small 11-room *logis* of the Doubs, with good reliable cooking and local dishes on menus priced from F56 to F110. Excellent value. Restaurant closed Tuesday except during July and August.

90000 Belfort

HOTEL LES CAPUCINS
29 Faubourg de Montbéliard
Territoire de Belfort
☎ (84) 28 04 60
This is the only *logis* in the territory of Belfort, the only part of France not to surrender to the Prussians in 1871. The hotel has 35 rooms and menus from F72 to F160. Very good food and highly recommended. Restaurant closed Saturday and Sunday outside high season.

25000 Besançon

LE BISTRO DU JURA
35 Rue Charles Nodier
☎ (81) 82 03 48

Very popular with the locals, which is always a good sign, this first-class restaurant has menus from F150 to F180. Highly recommmended.

TERRASSE HOTEL
36 Ave Carnot
☎ (81) 88 03 03
Besançon is a very fine city, well worth a full day's visit. This central 2-star *logis* has 36 rooms and sound menus priced from F60 to F120.

LA TOUR HENRIETTE
59 Faubourg de Besançon
Montbéliard
☎ (81) 91 03 24
A well-established and very friendly restaurant, usually full of local people. Traditional food to match the decor, so try the *filet de bar au gingembre*. Menus from F100 to F280. Highly recommended.

39300 Champagnole

HOTEL DU PARC
13 Rue Paul Cretin
☎ (84) 52 13 20
Mme Baron won the local round of the *Logis de France* Cookery Contest with her *coq-au-vin jaune*, so this place is well worth a visit. 20 rooms, menus (dinner only) from F60 to F160. The Hôtel du Parc is a good centre for exploring the lake district of the Jura and the hotel offers fishing in the River Ain, walking in the local forests and menus with local specialities cooked by the excellent Mme Baron – chicken, fish, mushrooms, snails, Jura wine. Recommended.

39200 St Claude

HOTEL ST HUBERT
3 Place St Hubert
☎ (84) 45 10 70
A good central *logis*, ideal for the Jura Massif, with 30 rooms and good, varied menus priced from F70 to F180. Closed Sunday, and Monday lunchtime.

25370 Les Hôpitaux-Neufs

HOTEL L'ETOILE DES NEIGES
4 Rue du Village
Métabief
☎ (81) 49 17 71
The Jura Massif is great for *ski-de-fond*, or cross-country skiing. This 1-star *logis* has 15 rooms and inexpensive menus from F58 to F98.

HOTEL ROBBE
Village centre
☎ (81) 49 11 05
A small hotel set 3000 ft up in Les Hôpitaux-Neufs. 20 rooms and adequate inexpensive menus priced from F55 to F80. Not refined cooking but good country fare.

39000 Lons-le-Saunier

RELAIS D'ALSACE
740 Route de Besançon
☎ (84) 47 24 70
You will dine well at M. Zorn's agreeable little restaurant on the road to Besançon. Try the *coquilles St Jacques au vin jaune*, a local speciality. Menus from F75 to F180.

HOTEL TERMINUS
37 Ave Aristide Briand
☎ (84) 24 41 83
A small central *logis* with just 18 rooms and very good menus, priced from F60 to F180. Lons-le-Saunier has five *logis*, but I recommend this one from personal experience.

25160 Malbuisson

HOTEL PARNET
Oye-et-Pallet
☎ (81) 89 42 03
A 3-star *logis* of the Doubs, with 18 rooms and good menus from F70 to F170. Restaurant closed Sunday evening and Monday.

39330 Mouchard

CHALET BEL-AIR HOTEL
Village centre
☎ (84) 37 80 34
Logis with just a few rooms tend to have good restaurants, and so it is here at Mouchard. The Châlet has just seven rooms but the restaurant serves first-class food on menus from F100 to F300. Excellent value. Restaurant closed Wednesday outside high season and Easter.

25290 Ornans

HOTEL DE FRANCE
51–53 Rue Pierre Vernier
☎ (81) 62 24 44

It would be impossible to visit the Jura without stopping at Ornans, the home of Courbet. This excellent *logis* on the River Loue has 31 rooms and excellent menus, priced from F100 to F250. Recommended. Restaurant closed Sunday evening and Monday outside high season.

39130 Pont-de-Poitte

HOTEL DE L'AIN
Clairvaux-les-Lacs
☎ (84) 48 30 16
A small *logis* of the Jura with just 10 rooms. Excellent food on menus from F80 to F250 that include many local dishes. A very pretty spot. Restaurant closed Sunday evening and Monday outside high season.

39220 Les Rousses

CHEZ ARBEZ
La Cure
☎ (84) 60 02 20
Set right on the Franco-Swiss frontier, this pleasant restaurant offers excellent cheese and local dishes on an excellent F89 menu. Other menus available from F150 to F230. Recommended.

RELAIS DES GENTIANES
309 Rue Pasteur
☎ (84) 60 50 64
Les Rousses is a ski and walking centre for the Jura with several good *logis*. This one has 14 rooms and good menus from F85 to F220. Try the *truite au vin jaune*. Recommended as a stopping place for walkers on the GR5 footpath.

25800 Valdahon

RELAIS DE FRANCHE-COMTE
Rue Charles Schmitt
☎ (81) 56 23 18
A very good *logis* of the Doubs, worth a diversion for the scenery and the excellent menus ranging from F52 to F200. Local dishes and local wines from Arbois. 20 rooms. Highly recommended. Restaurant closed Friday evening and Saturday except February, July and August.

70240 Velleminfroy

HOSTELLERIE DU CHATEAU-GRENOUILLE
Village centre
Saulx
☎ (84) 74 30 11
The name itself will draw visitors to this small auberge of the Haute
Saône. The village has only 200 people, the hotel only seven rooms,
but the food is excellent and the F140 menu a real *tour de force*.

70000 Vesoul

HOTEL AUX VENDANGES DE BOURGOGNE
49 Boulevard de Gaulle
☎ (84) 75 81 21
A large *logis* with 30 rooms and good, reliable menus priced from F65
to F130. Local dishes and a wide range of wines, some from Arbois.
Restaurant closed from mid August to early September.

POITOU-CHARENTES

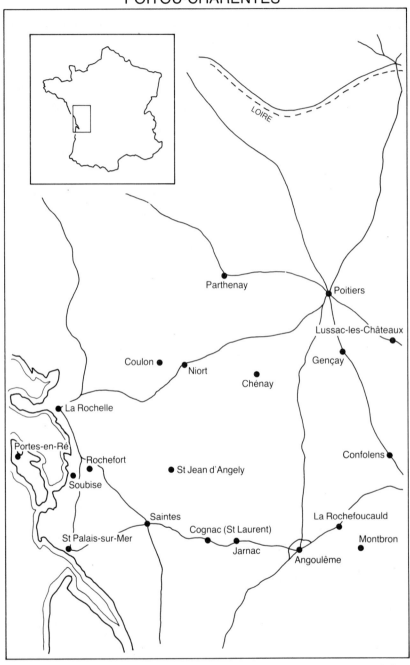

POITOU-
CHARENTES

I once ate three dozen oysters at a sitting in the town of La Rochelle. Not in one go, I grant you, but 12 at a time, which is still rather a lot. I was with some friends and we had a dozen apiece, and they were rather good, so we had another 12, and then – what the hell! – another 12. The seafood of the Poitou-Charentes region is delicious, and I speak here of what I know. If you like oysters, crab, lobster or any form of seafood, you will find it at its finest here.

Poitou-Charentes, sometimes called Western France, lies south of the Loire and the Vendée region and is bordered on the east by the Limousin, and on the south by Aquitaine and the Périgord. Modern Poitou-Charentes is composed of four *départements*, Deux-Sèvres, Vienne, Charente and Charente-Maritime. Access from the north is easy, with the entire region within a day's drive across Brittany from the western Channel ports.

Scenically, the land lacks drama, but the coastline is magnificent, with glorious beaches further improved by a number of offshore islands, such as the Ile de Ré and the Ile d'Oléron. Further south, past Royan, the coastline forms the northern shore of the Gironde estuary, a region of sandflats and mudbanks, a paradise for birds. The main physical feature of the landscape lies inland and further north, near Niort, in the *Venise Verte*, the 'Green Venice' of the Marais Poitevin, a kind of placid, Gallic fenland, of marshes and meadows and canals, where everything moves by punt. There are also a number of very attractive rivers, such as the Vienne and the Charente, and many attractive towns. The land is bathed in warm sunlight during the summer and autumn, with just enough rain to keep everything green and with all this to offer, as well as good food, it is surprising to find Poitou-Charentes largely unvisited by foreign travellers, although the region is extremely popular with the French.

Visitors from the north might come in via Loudun and so into the Vienne via the town of Poitiers, where the Black Prince beat King Jean in 1356. The battlefield lies near Nouaille-Maupertius, 9 miles south-east of the city. Poitiers is an attractive town and has many connections with England, as it was once the capital of Aquitaine, in the days of Henry II and Richard Coeur-de-Lion. To the west of Poitiers lies the town of Parthenay, a stopping place on the Road to Compostela and full of medieval buildings, with a notable fortified bridge. Parthenay should be remembered by all true travellers as the home of a monk, Améri Picaud, who made the pilgrimage to Compostela about the year 1120 and wrote a book about the journey, the *Libris Sancti Jacobi*, which is said to be the world's first guidebook. On the River Vienne, which gives its name to this *département*, there are two attractive towns. The first is Châtellerault, which is actually two towns joined by a single bridge. Here there is a church dedicated to St James – St Jacques – and the shops sell the sort of cutlery that should adorn any serious kitchen. The other town, Chauvigny, is also a manufacturing centre, but here they make jugs and porcelain. The ruins of the castle occupy the town centre, but the finest castle hereabouts is the one at Touffou, 4 miles to the north.

The capital of the Charente is Angoulême, on the River Charente, with the old town still within the walls of the medieval *cité*, set high above the plain. The twelfth-century church of St Pierre in Angoulême has a magnificent typanum and the whole town is worth exploring before heading down the river towards the coast, through the cognac country. The town of Cognac is full of cellars, many of the *chais* of the cognac distilleries such as Hine and Courvoisier, most of which can be visited. Saintes, further downstream, is also worth closer inspection, for it contains a splendid Roman amphitheatre of the first century AD and a triumphal arch dedicated to Germanicus. The old town on the left bank of the river is a maze of narrow medieval streets, and the town has a number of good restaurants.

And so to the coast. La Rochelle was once a stronghold of the Huguenot Protestants until it was captured by forces commanded by Cardinal Richelieu in 1628, though there is still a large Protestant community. La Rochelle is now a major fishing port and very picturesque, as is the little town of Rochefort, the home of the writer Pierre Loti, which now doubles as a spa. The offshore islands can all be visited, but if I had to choose one spot along this coast where visitors rarely venture, I would suggest a trip to the fortress town of Brouage, south of Rochefort, which stands all alone on the flatlands. It was built by Richelieu to command and protect the valuable salt-pans, and is slowly sinking into the marsh, but as a prime example of seventeenth-century military architecture it cannot be missed. Inland from here lies Pons, another stop on the Road to Compostela, and you can see the statues of two saints in pilgrim garb in the little church at Avy.

One should roam about in Poitou-Charentes, for there is a lot to see. Barbézieux is a cognac centre, Loudun was the scene of a famous trial for witchcraft, later portrayed by Aldous Huxley in his book *The Devils of Loudun*, but if you like something less mentally testing, there are plenty of pleasant seaside resorts, such as Royan and Mortagne, along the Gironde estuary.

Essential sights

The towns of Poitiers, La Rochelle and Angoulême, are all worth visiting. The 1356 Battlefield at Poitiers. The fortress of Brouage. Spend a day or two floating about the canals of the *Venise Verte*. Visit the *chais* in Cognac, and the hilltown of Pons, and see the Porte St Jacques at Parthenay.

Food

You can sometimes find local caviar at Mortagne-sur-Gironde, for the sturgeon still come into the river and are caught for their eggs, called *créat* hereabouts. Oysters, lobsters and all kinds of crustaceans can be found at their best along the coast, and the rich wetlands of the Marais provide the wherewithal for excellent beef and *pré-salé* lamb and mutton. The local fish is excellent, and includes, apart from trout and salmon, tuna and sardines, eels from the Marais, oysters from Marennes, mussels from La Rochelle, where a typical dish is La Chaudrée, a fish soup. Curnousky, 'Le Prince des Gastronomes', described Charantaise cooking as 'honest and direct', and this still holds good today, although butter and cream are much in evidence with the sauces. The fruit and vegetables are excellent, and there are few things nicer than a plump Charentais melon, but there is no local cheese other than the goat's cheese – *chabichou* – of Poitou.

Wine

Most of the local grapes are used for the production of cognac, although there is a local aperitif called *pineau de Charentes*. If you want a good cognac after your meal, it is simpler to ask for a *fine* rather than plunge into a mass of marques and vintages. The only wine comes from Haut-Poitou, from the co-operative at Neuville, which produces a VDQS red, white and rosé, quite palatable. Otherwise it is Muscadet to complement the seafood, or a good claret from further south.

RESTAURANTS

16000 Angoulême

HOTEL LA BOURSE
Place Gérard-Pérot
☎ (45) 92 06 42
M. Rolland, who has run this fine hotel for many years and won prizes for his cuisine, has it in mind to sell, and we hope that the new owner will maintain existing standards. 29 rooms, menus from F50 to F200. Currently recommended.

MARCO-POLO
18 Rue des Trois Notre-Dame
☎ (45) 92 53 11
The chef here has recently changed but Mlle Haccoun maintains a good table with local dishes like *mouclade Charentaise au pineau* and a splendid *plateau fruits de mer*. Menus at F75 plus a good *carte*. Recommended.

79120 Chénay

HOTEL LES TROIS PIGEONS
Lézay
☎ (49) 07 38 59
A hotel of Deux-Sèvres, with 12 rooms and menus well supplied with Poitouvin dishes priced from F57 to F140. A pleasant restaurant and an agreeable hotel. Restaurant closed Friday evening and Saturday.

16100 Cognac (St Laurent)

LOGIS DE BEAULIEU
Route Nationale 141
St Laurent-de-Cognac
☎ (45) 82 30 50
A good place to stay while touring the *chais*. 21 rooms, local dishes and menus sensibly priced from F120 to F160. This hotel offers very good food with sauces with just a hint of the local specific.

16500 Confolens

LA TOUR DE NESLE
3 Rue de la Côte
☎ (45) 84 03 70
The food here is simple, without great flourishes or heaps of cream, but very good and served with a warm smile. Menus from F62 to F146, and an excellent wine list, with a great selection of Loire vintages.

HOTEL DE VIENNE
4 Rue de la Ferrandie
☎ (45) 84 09 24
Mme Dupré runs this little 14-room *logis*, in one of the most agreeable towns in the Charente, a very pleasant stop on the road south across France. Menus from F52 to F125 in a restaurant with rather erratic opening hours, though it tends to be closed most Friday evenings and open at other times.

79270 Coulon

HOTEL LE CENTRAL
4 Rue d'Autremont
☎ (49) 35 90 20
A good *logis* with just seven rooms and good, traditional menus ranging from F72 to F152. It bears repeating that you tend to eat better in small hotels, and here you will eat very well from the F95 menu. Restaurant closed Sunday evening and Monday.

HOTEL AU MARAIS
48 Quai Tardy
☎ (49) 35 90 43
Slightly larger than the Central, with 11 rooms, this good *logis* has menus from F75 to F150. Either hotel would be a good base while exploring the Marais Poitevin, which should not be missed on any visit to this part of France.

86160 Gençay

HOTEL DU GUESCLIN
Rue Carnot
☎ (49) 59 33 53
A good stop on the road south, a few miles south of Poitiers. Only 10 rooms, so it is best to look. Good, reliable menus from F42 to F82.

16200 Jarnac

CHATEAU DE FLEURAC
On N141 at Fleurac
☎ (45) 35 82 17
Most château-restaurants are long on décor but short on value. This one has good menus from F120 to F150. Try it. 18 rooms.

RESTAURANT DU CHATEAU
Place du Château
☎ (45) 81 07 17
This unpretentious little restaurant is ideal for lunch. *Escalope jarnaçaise à la crème* may go down well after your visit to the Courvoisier cellars opposite. Menus from F68 to F125.

HOTEL TERMINUS
Ave Carnot
☎ (45) 81 07 04
Jarnac is a pleasant town, close to the Cognac district, and this hotel would be a good place to stay while eating and drinking in the surrounding countryside. There are 12 rooms and good-value menus priced from F55 to F140. Restaurant closed Friday evening and Saturday outside high season.

17400 St Jean d'Angely

HOTEL LE CHALET
66 Ave Aristide Briand
☎ (46) 32 01 08
A very fine town with two good *logis*. This one has 19 rooms, and good menus ranging from F45 to F110.

86320 Lussac-les-Châteaux

LE RELAIS
Town centre
☎ (49) 48 40 20
The Black Prince's great captain, John Chandos, was killed by the bridge at Lussac, and you can find his tomb behind the houses on the left of the road up from the river. This *relais* on the banks of the Vienne, is an *auberge* with eight rooms and menus from F47 to F170. Restaurant closed Sunday evening and Monday, except during during July and August.

16220 Montbron

CHATEAU STE CATHERINE
South of Montbron on D36
☎ (45) 23 60 03
Set in its own park, this 18-room hotel offers excellent value, with menus sensibly priced from F125 to F200. The food leans towards fish and *cuisine moderne* – but not quite *nouvelle* – and the setting is superb. Worth trying.

RELAIS DES TROIS-MARCHANDS
10 Rue de Limoges
☎ (45) 70 71 29
If the château-hotel fails to appeal, this excellent *logis* in the town has 11 rooms and good menus well spaced from F50 to F160. Restaurant closed Sunday evening and Monday.

79000 Niort

HOTEL TERMINUS – LA POELE D'OR
82 Rue de La Gare
☎ (49) 24 00 38
If you can't find a hotel, head for the railway station – there are usually a couple around there in most towns, but few are as good as the Terminus, which serves local dishes on menus from F70 to F160. Niort is a good place to stay while touring the *Venise Verte*, the green marshland of Poitou, just to the west. 40 rooms. Restaurant closed Saturday.

17420 St Palais-sur-Mer

HOTEL DE LA PLAGE
1 Place de l'Océan
☎ (46) 23 10 32
This resort at the northern mouth of the Gironde, facing the wide Atlantic, is just off the beaten track. The hotel has 29 rooms and a good reputation for food. Menus priced from F80 to F250. Recommended for those who prefer the coast to the countryside.

79200 Parthenay

HOTEL DU NORD
86 Ave Général de Gaulle
☎ (49) 94 29 11
This hotel is one of three *logis* in this old town in Deux-Sèvres, with just 13 rooms but good local dishes with menus priced from F52 to

F160. Try the *côte de boeuf*. Parthenay has a magnificent fortified gateway, through which pilgrims set out on the Road to Compostela, and the entire town is quite beautiful and greatly overlooked.

86000 Poitiers

HOTEL DE PARIS
123 Boulevard du Grand Cerf
☎ (49) 58 39 37
There is a cluster of hotels in the Grand Cerf, but this one, with 10 rooms, is the one with good dishes and an excellent wine list. It is best to book in summer. Menus from F58 to F125.

17880 Portes-en-Ré

AUBERGE DE LA RIVIERE
Ave de Salins
D 101 La Rivière
Ile de Ré
☎ (46) 29 54 55
Oysters, fish, good local dishes, sensible menus with good wine and a pleasant welcome combine to make this *auberge* one of the best restaurants on the Ile de Ré. Menus from F80 to F180. Recommended.

17300 Rochefort

HOTEL LE PARIS
27–29 Ave Lafayette
☎ (46) 99 33 11
Rochefort is a beautiful little town, popular with artists. It draws people back year after year, not least because as a fishing port its restaurants can make good use of the produce hauled fresh from the Atlantic. This is a large *logis*, with 40 rooms, but in July and August be sure to book. The restaurant offers good food on a range of menus from F70 to F140.

LE TOURNE-BROCHE
56 Ave du Général de Gaulle
☎ (46) 99 20 19
A good restaurant serving excellent seafood from well-chosen menus. Try the *huîtres chaudes à la crème d'ail*, or the *jambon de Vendée*. Menus from F75 to F95, plus *carte*. Good wine list.

16110 La Rochefoucauld

LA VIEILLE AUBERGE
13 Faubourg La Souche
☎ (45) 62 02 72
A pleasant hotel in this very agreeable old town, with 28 rooms and menus priced from F50 to F185. Friendly staff.

17000 La Rochelle

LA MARMITE
14 Rue St Jean-du-Pérot
☎ (46) 41 17 03
A good, reliable seafood restaurant with a Michelin rosette, one of several in the town with this distinction. Good sole, fine, succulent oysters, lobster. Menus from F150 to F330 – not cheap, but first-class; the place for a memorable meal.

86600 Rosignons

HOTEL DU CHAPEAU ROUGE
1 Route Nationale
Lusignan
☎ (49) 43 31 10
One of two good *logis* in Lusignan – the other is the Promenades on the Avenue de Poitou. This hotel has eight rooms and sound menus priced from F60 to F130. Recommended.

17100 Saintes

LE LOGIS SANTON
54 Cours Genet
☎ (46) 74 20 14
Excellent food, not simply seafood, in this fine, traditional restaurant, expertly managed by Mme Sorillet. Menus from F85 to F155, a first-class range of good Bordeaux wines, and – of course – cognac. Highly recommended.

17780 Soubise

LA SOUBISE
62 Rue de la République
☎ (46) 84 93 36
In a village 8 miles from Rochefort, this excellent restaurant, run by René Benoît, offers first-class food and an excellent wine list at very bearable prices, with a good F145 menu. Worth a long detour and highly recommended.

LIMOUSIN

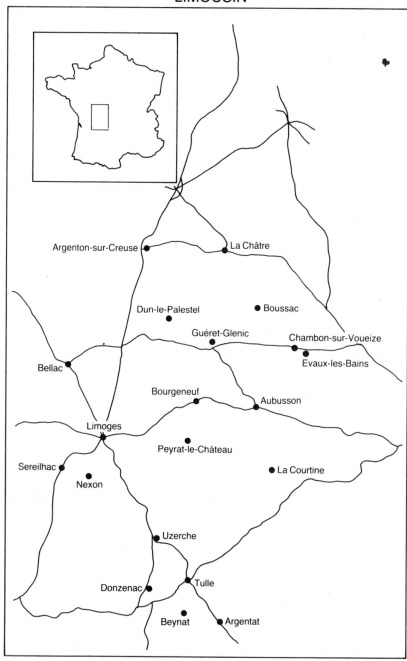

LIMOUSIN

The Limousin is one of the lesser-known areas of France, perhaps because most foreigners are unaware of it, or perhaps because it has been overwhelmed by the charms of the Dordogne and Périgord, which lie no great distance to the south. The capital of the Limousin, Limoges, is best known for porcelain, although in France it is almost as well known for having the prettiest girls in the entire country. I cannot vouch for this personally, but the French are said to know about such things.

The Limousin is a tight little region, made up of three *départements*, Haute-Vienne, Creuse and Corrèze. Scenically the Limousin is much gentler than the Auvergne to the east or the Périgord country further south. This is an area of lakes and green, forested hills, small towns and smaller villages. The access for most visitors will be from the north, with many British visitors racing through the Limousin on their way to the Dordogne, which they have practically recolonized in recent years. This route usually brings them in via Bellac, north of Limoges, but one stop near here, which might sadden the heart, is the ruined village of Oradour-sur-Glane, which was totally destroyed by the 2nd SS Division (Das Reich) in the summer of 1944, when most of the inhabitants were murdered. I'm not suggesting that this ruined village is a tourist attraction, simply that what happened there should not be forgotten.

Limoges is a very fine city, but to prove that no one nation has a monopoly of destruction, the Black Prince and his knights massacred the population here during the Hundred Years War. Limoges still makes porcelain and the works can be visited, but my advice is to park near the Cathedral of St Etienne and just stroll about the narrow streets and houses of this attractive city. South of Limoges lies Solignac, with its beautiful abbey, and then comes Uzerche on the Vézère, a curious little town, because many of the older houses look like castles. I like castles, which may be why I like Uzerche. Further south still lies another fine little town, Turenne, near Brive, with a great tower, the Tour de César, overtopping the roofs. But to stay within the broad confines of the Limousin, one must turn north through the Corrèze, past the great lake at Vassivière, and over the beautiful Millevaches plateau, which refers not to cows, but to the thousand springs which are said to rise here. Aubusson on the Creuse is a tapestry centre, and still retains its medieval centre. From here the valley of the Creuse leads north to Guéret, a very fine town, and as one might expect, quite small, with a population of less than 18,000. The Limousin is a place to roam about in, for it lies off the popular tourist track and is not very large. If you like good country cooking and very pleasant people, this is the region to explore.

Essential sights

Limoges, a very fine city. Turenne, set in more rugged country, with many old houses and the relics of a medieval castle. The Millevaches plateau is ideal for walkers, and places such as Aubusson and Argenton-sur-Creuse are fine little towns with good hotels. Oradour-sur-Glane can hardly be missed.

Food

The food in the Limousin, like the land itself, is less simple, perhaps rather more refined than that of the Auvergne, while not yet as rich as that of Périgord, although *pâté de foie gras* can certainly be found here. Food *à la Limousin* is prepared with chestnuts, onions or red cabbage and, increasingly, *cèpes*. Local pâtés often include chestnuts or even truffles. Mushrooms appear in many dishes, especially omelettes, and there are more mushroom varieties here than are currently found in Britain, so look out for the slender *chanterelles*, the *cèpes* and the *morels*. The local meat, beef and pork, is excellent, and there are several locally produced cheeses, such as the Guéret, a cow's-milk cheese from the Millevaches plateau. The local dessert is *clafoutis*, a cherry batter pudding.

Wine

There is no local wine in the Limousin, but the region draws in

*Tympanum of St Pierre,
Aulnay, Poitou-Charentes*

Argentat in the Dordogne

Murol in the Auvergne

Monts de Cantal, in the Auvergne

Lac Merlet, Courcheval, in the French Alps (photo: Annie Scheider)

Villard-de-Lans on the Vercors plateau

Les Arcs in the Alps

vintages from the country round about, so the wine lists you find in the restaurants tend to be both full and varied.

RESTAURANTS

19400 Argentat

HOTEL GILBERT
Rue Vachal
☎ (55) 28 01 62
A pretty little town of the Corrèze, off the tourist route but worth the detour. Argentat offers three *logis*, but I recommend this one for its warm welcome. 27 rooms, so you can usually get in, and good menus from F65 to F180. Try the local fish and pâtés. Restaurant closed Friday evening and Saturday.

36200 Argenton-sur-Creuse

HOTEL LE CHEVAL-NOIR
27 Rue Auclert-Descottes
☎ (54) 24 00 06
A central *logis* with good parking and pleasant people. Good menus from F75 to F160. 30 rooms. Restaurant closed Monday.

HOTEL DE FRANCE
8 Rue de J.-J. Rousseau
☎ (54) 24 03 31
Another winner of the *Logis de France* Cookery Contest, when Michel Ramon swept the board with his succulent *coq au vin*. 22 rooms. Menus from F56 to F108. Highly recommended.

CHEZ MAITRE JEAN
67 Ave Rollmat
☎ (54) 24 02 09
This little *auberge*, with just six rooms, is more of a restaurant than an hotel and is mentioned in the Michelin Guide. Menus from F50 to F110. Restaurant closed Wednesday.

23200 Aubusson

HOTEL DE FRANCE
Town centre
☎ (55) 66 10 22

The famous tapestries bring visitors to this town of the Creuse, but the whole area, full of pretty places, is well worth seeing. The Hôtel de France has 20 rooms and M. Dubreuil makes a point of including regional recipes in his menus, which run from F60 to a *gastronomique* at F200. Recommended.

19390 St Augustin

AUBERGE DES BRUYERES
Chaumeil
☎ (55) 21 34 68
Marcelle Feugeas won the Regional Cookery Contest in 1987 when his *ris de veau aux cèpes*, and keeps up the standards in his 15-room *auberge*, with good food on menus from F55 to F120. Recommended.

87300 Bellac

HOTEL LES CHATAIGNIERS
Route de Poitiers
☎ (55) 68 14 82
Set a little outside the town, this 2-star *logis* has 27 rooms and good, varied menus from F88 to F220. A good stopping place on the road to or from the Dordogne. Restaurant closed Sunday evening and Monday.

19190 Beynat

HOTEL LE TOURTEL
Town centre
☎ (55) 85 50 28
The Corrèze is a beautiful and little-visited part of France, best explored from a base in Beynat, and where better to stay than Le Tourtel. 10 rooms, pleasant people, and good, inexpensive menus from F65 to F120.

19110 Bort-les-Orgues

CENTRAL HOTEL
Ave de la Gare
☎ (55) 96 74 82
The lake and castle, the famous and photogenic Château du Val, draw visitors to Bort, but the Central will keep them there for a day or two. 25 rooms, excellent food on menus from F79 to F175.

23400 Bourgeneuf

HOTEL-RESTAURANT LE COMMERCE
12 Rue de Verdun
☎ (55) 64 14 55
A very fine 2-star *logis* in the town centre where M. Jabet has been serving good food for over 50 years – he started cooking at 13. If he likes you, he will take you home and show you his confections made in icing sugar, but his menus are also excellent and range from F60 to F220. 16 rooms. Restaurant closed Sunday evening and Monday.

23600 Boussac

LE BOEUF COURONNE
Place de l'Hôtel de Ville
☎ (55) 65 15 92
Another stopping place on my walk across France in 1987, where a warm welcome excused my late arrival. A nice town of La Marche in the north of the Creuse, and well worth a visit. 11 rooms and inexpensive menus from F45 to F90.

19100 Brive

LA CREMAILLERIE
53 Ave de Paris
☎ (55) 74 32 47
One of several *logis* in Brive, on one of the main routes to the Dordogne and the Lot, this excellent 10-room hotel serves local dishes with menus from F130 to F220. Restaurant closed Sunday evening and Monday.

HOTEL LE MONTAUBAN
6 Ave Edouard-Herriot
☎ (55) 24 00 38
This *logis* serving local specialities in its sunny restaurant is in the town centre, but you can park. 18 rooms and menus from F60 to F120. Worth a stop.

19240 Brive-Varetz

CHATEAU DE CASTEL NOVEL
At Varetz on D152
☎ (55) 85 00 01
This is that rarity, a 4-star *logis* with all the appropriate trimmings, such as a swimming pool, but serving local dishes on good menus from F190 to F370. Not cheap but excellent value, and not actually in

Brive but in the village of Varetz, some miles to the north. Well worth a diversion, and highly recommended if you want to splash out.

23170 Chambon-sur-Voueize

HOTEL ESTONNERIES
41 Ave Clemenceau
☎ (55) 82 14 66
A small hotel of the Creuse, with just 12 rooms, but good menus priced in the middle range from F90 to F170. Recommended.

136400 La Châtre

HOTEL LES TANNERIES
2 Rue du Lion d'Argent
☎ (54) 48 21 00
A very pleasant, modern hotel with a rather chic restaurant and very comfortable rooms, set on the banks of the river. 10 rooms and excellent food on menus from F100 to F250. I stayed here one Saturday night on my walk across France, looking rather odd in boots and anorak, among the other, more elegant diners. Recommended.

23100 La Courtine

HOTEL-RESTAURANT AU PETIT BREUIL
Plazanet-Gourgues
Route de Felletin
☎ (55) 66 76 67
A small, highly recommended *logis* with just nine rooms, but excellent food on menus from F45 to F180. Well worth a detour, because this little town is set in the most beautiful rolling countryside, quite off the beaten track.

19270 Donzenac

HOTEL LA GAMADE
Place Léon Madrias
☎ (55) 85 71 07
Donzenac, a little north of Brive-la-Gaillarde, has two good *logis* – the other is the Relais Bas Limousin on the N20. This one has 10 rooms and Mme Salesse's good country cooking. Menus from F60 to F170. Recommended.

23800 Dun-le-Palestel

HOTEL JOLY
Village centre
☎ (55) 89 00 23
Dun is a small town in the northern Creuse, north-west of Guéret. The Joly is a long-established hotel where M. Monceaux offers a very good menu for just F45 and others rising to F190, so not expensive. The F55 menu has won recent praise for the braised ham in *sauce madère*. 12 rooms. Restaurant closed Saturday evening and Monday lunchtime.

23110 Evaux-les-Bains

HOTEL CHARDONNET
18 Rue de l'Hôtel de Ville
☎ (55) 65 51 78
As the name implies, Evaux is a spa, and rather full of elderly people. You will eat well at this 1-star *logis* from menus pitched between F50 and F155. 27 rooms. Restaurant closed Sunday evening.

23380 Guéret-Glenic

LE MOULIN NOYE
Ajain
☎ (55) 52 09 11
Guéret is a resort town of the Creuse, a great walking and fishing centre, with this excellent 2-star *logis* as a centrepiece. 18 rooms and excellent choices of local food on menus from F62 to the *gastronomique* at F185. Recommended for good food and proximity to the beautiful Millevaches plateau.

87000 Limoges

LE MARCEAU
2 Ave de Turenne
☎ (55) 77 23 43
Unlike most large French cities, Limoges (pop. 150,000) has no less than five *logis*, from which I have selected two (this one and The Belvedere in the Rue de Toulouse). Le Marceau has 13 rooms and local dishes on menus priced from F55 to F200, offering a wide price range. Restaurant closed Sunday.

LE TROU NORMAND
1 Rue François Chénieux
☎ (55) 77 53 24

A curious name for a restaurant of the Limousin, but Mme Métails comes from Honfleur. Even so, fish gives way here to good grills and tournedos. Excellent wines. *Carte* only, say F250 per head.

87800 Nexon

MOULIN DE LA GORCE
On D17 south of Nexon
Roche-L'Abeille
☎ (55) 00 70 66
This restaurant occupies a seventeenth-century mill, outside Nexon south of Limoges. 9 rooms only, so food is the great draw, with the wine list a good second. This pretty restaurant by the lake has two Michelin rosettes and offers too many excellent dishes to mention, on menus from F200 to F400. Not cheap perhaps, but well worth the visit. Restaurant closed Sunday evening and Monday outside high season.

87470 Peyrat-le-Château

AUBERGE DU BOIS DE L'ETANG
Rue de la Tour
☎ (55) 69 40 19
A large *logis* by the lake, with 31 rooms and offering *bonne table et bon accueil*, which translates roughly as fine cooking, local specialities and reasonable prices. Menus from F68 to F180. Recommended.

87620 Sereilhac

MOTEL DES TUILERIES
Les Bétoulles
☎ (55) 39 10 27
Do not let the name put you off this *logis*, on the road to the Dordogne south-east of Limoges. Only 10 rooms, but good food with local dishes on menus from F60 to F200. Restaurant closed Sunday night and Monday.

36160 Ste Sevère-sur-Indre

L'ECU DE FRANCE
25 Rue d'Auvergne
☎ (54) 30 52 72
Although it lies a little outside the northern limit of the Creuse *département*, this little hotel-restaurant can be fitted in on the way north from Boussac. M. Blanchet is a noted local chef and lunch or

dinner in his delightful dining room is a real treat. Seven rooms. Menus from F56 to F130. Closed Monday.

19000 Tulle

HOTEL ST MARTIN
45 Quai Aristide Briand
☎ (55) 26 12 18
Tulle was the site of a terrible massacre by the Waffen SS in 1944, but is now again a pretty town of Corrèze, famous for thin veils – in *tulle*, of course. This *logis*, one of two in the town, is the one that serves local food. 24 rooms. Menus from F60 to F120. Recommended.

19140 Uzerche

HOTEL SAGNE
Town centre
☎ (55) 73 17 75
This is an *auberge*, with 17 rooms and local dishes on inexpensive menus from F52 to F120. A useful hotel in a good stopping place on the road south.

AUVERGNE

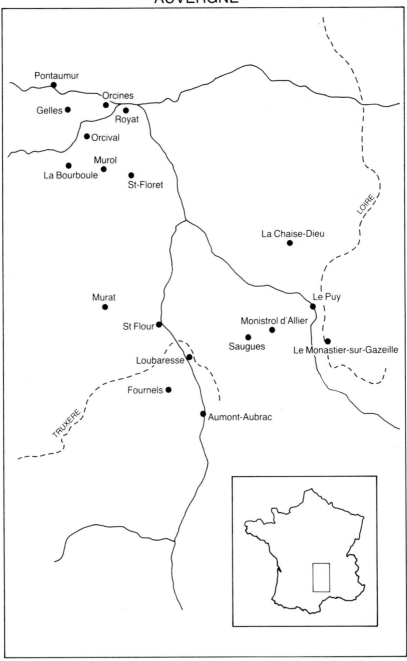

Pontaumur

Orcines

Gelles ●

Royat

● Orcival

Murol

La Bourboule ●

St-Floret

LOIRE

La Chaise-Dieu ●

Murat ●

Le Puy

St Flour ●

Monistrol d'Allier ●

Saugues ●

Le Monastier-sur-Gazeille ●

Loubaresse ●

Fournels ●

TRUXERE

Aumont-Aubrac ●

AUVERGNE

Just to declare an interest, may I state that the Auvergne is my favourite part of France. I have walked across it and cycled round it and motored through it, and I go there as often as I can because the Auvergne is both beautiful and quite unspoiled. Much of this present province is the ancient Bourbonnais, and the Auvergne countryside has become increasingly empty in recent years as the people give up the land and leave to work in the cities. The Auvergne – the Massif Central – is a volcanic, mountainous province, with few large towns and many small villages, a country of farmers, often sheep farmers, though there is a wild breed of Auvergne cattle which have given me an unpleasant turn or two. That apart, the countryside is virtually empty.

Inevitably in such a poor province there is little one can recognize as gastronomy, but there are good local dishes and at least one excellent local wine, St Porçain, so all is not lost. It may be that the local food is enhanced by the fact that most people exploring the Auvergne do so on foot or by bicycle, and come hungry to the table, but one can easily find good, traditional, provincial cooking in this beautiful part of France, and the land is worth exploring anyway.

Auvergne contains four *départements* – Allier, Haute-Loire, Puy-de-Dôme, and my personal favourite, Cantal. The access here is from the north, across the Loire, or from the east, the Rhône Valley. Coming in from the north, Montluçon is the first town of any size, though it is a modern town on the River Cher, with a small ancient *quartier* on the right bank to add a little charm. The chief attraction of the town is the fifteenth-century castle of the Dukes of Bourbon, which is now a museum. Moving south, Clermont-Ferrand is the home of Michelin and therefore industrial, but to the east of the town glorious country opens up at once with the long chain of the Monts de Dôme. This is the 'volcano country' of Central France, a moonscape of soft-coned hills and lake-filled craters, more than 80 in all, running south to and past the Monts Dore, as far as the Monts du Cantal. I have walked south across this country and can recommend Orcival and the beautiful château of Cordes nearby as places to visit. Le Mont Dore is a ski resort and spa at the foot of the mountains, and other good places to visit hereabouts include La Bourboule, Lac Chambon, Bort-les-Orgues and the classic Château de Val, set on the lake nearby. Just across the Monts Dore lies Besse-en-Chandesse, a medieval town, and nearby lies Lac Pavin, a beautiful, blue, circular lake, set in a volcanic crater, like so many of those lakes in the area. This is stunning country, and it gets even better as you move south through Egliseneuve d'Entraigues, to the next range of mountains, the Monts de Cantal, and the resort of Lioran, at the foot of the Plomb du Cantal. Lioran is modern, but surrounded by stunning scenery and fine little villages.

East of here, across the Planèze, the plateau of Cantal, lies the hilltop city of St Flour, which has at least two excellent restaurants, and to the south lies the wilderness of the Aubrac plateau, above the valley of the Lot. Go east and you will cross the Allier and arrive at the pilgrim city of Le Puy and the green Vélay country, with the Abbey at La Chaise Dieu and the castle of Polignac, a little north of Le Puy as just two impressive sights. South of Le Puy lies the little town of Le Monastier-sur-Gazeille, from where Robert Louis Stevenson set out on his *Travels with a Donkey in the Cévennes*, and close by lies the castle at Arlempedes, high above the rushing, infant Loire.

You can roam about the Auvergne for weeks like this, stopping at pretty places. The time to arrive is in the late spring, say May, when the meadows will be full of wild daffodils and the snow has gone from all but the tops of the mountains. The Auvergne is wildly beautiful and I urge you to see it.

Essential sights

There are so many good places in the Auvergne that I hardly know where to start. However, St Flour in Cantal is a very fine city, and Orcival has a magnificent cathedral. Nearby lies the little castle at Cordes, a Renaissance jewel. I love the Aubrac, south of St Flour, and the village of St Juéry and the castle at Allueze are worth seeking out in this area. The *Chaîne des Volcans* from the Puy de Dôme to the Monts Dore are quite stunning, as is Lac Pavin and the city of Le Puy.

Food

On my walk across the Auvergne, the otherwise hospitable hoteliers did put one barrier in my path by insisting that I tried their *tripaux*, which is various parts of sheep, including the feet, wrapped and cooked in the sheep's stomach. As I said earlier, entrails are not to my taste. The local dishes tend to be of the hearty variety, with lots of potatoes and vegetables, but I can certainly recommend the *salade Auvergnat*, which has mountain ham mixed with lettuce and onions. They also do good thick soups and substantial omelettes, while the lakes and rivers provide good trout and there is even salmon available at Brioude, although the speciality of Brioude is thrush pâté. The area has excellent, even famous cheeses, such as the *fourme de Cantal*, the *Bleu d'Auvergne*, the *St Nectaire*. Among other dishes, look out for *aligot*, creamed potatoes with bacon, onions and cheese, found on the Aubrac and elsewhere, which goes straight to your hips. *Oeufs à l'Auvergnat* is poached eggs with cabbage and potatoes, two ingredients which appear in any *à l'Auvergnat* recipe. The *friand de St Flour*, sausage-meat enclosed in cabbage leaves, can actually be delicious on a cold day, while in the northern Auvergne, the Bourbonnais, they do *oyonnade*, goose stew. On the pudding front, cherry tart seems the most popular, but the locals have a sweet tooth, so most restaurants offer a wide range of tarts and trifles.

Wine

The VDQS wines of St Porçain are the most common and very drinkable local wines, and available as red, white or rosé. The Côtes d'Auvergne wines have a good dry rosé, Corent, but my own practice was either to drink last year's St Porçain, or ask for a *pichet* of the house wine, which is never less than adequate and often very palatable. Other local wines which may appear on the list are the commune wines from Madargues and Boudes, and there is a very pleasant, inexpensive VDQS wine from the hills around Rodez in the south, called Marcillac.

RESTAURANTS

48130 Aumont-Aubrac

HOTEL PROUHEZE
Opposite the station
☎ (66) 42 80 07
The Aubrac is probably my favourite part of France, a wild plateau above the Lot Valley, south of St Fleur and actually just in Lozère, although it fits more naturally into the Auvergne. This excellent hotel is not cheap but has first-class food and wine and a Michelin rosette. Try the F150 menu for some excellent dishes.

63610 Besse-et-Ste-Anastaise

HOSTELLERIE DU BEFFROY
Town centre
☎ (73) 79 50 08
This is a ski centre in winter and a paradise for walkers in the late spring and summer, set in the volcano country east of the Monts Dore. Besse is a fortified town, very historic, and this hotel, one of several *logis* in the town, has 16 rooms and good food on menus from F63 to F200. Recommended.

63150 La Bourboule

HOTEL DU PARC
Quai Maréchal Fayolle
Town centre
☎ (73) 81 01 77
La Bourboule is a popular holiday resort of the Monts Dore in Cantal, and full of good hotels. This one serves excellent food, including local dishes. Not expensive, with menus from F70 to F120. 50 rooms.

43160 La Chaise-Dieu

HOTEL ECHO-ET-ABBAYE
Town centre
☎ (71) 00 00 45
The great monastery, with its *danse macabre* wall paintings, will bring most visitors to this little town in Haute-Loire, also an excellent walking and cross-country-skiing centre. This *logis* serves local fare and has menus from F80 to F220. 11 rooms. Restaurant closed Monday, except during high season.

63320 St-Floret-Champeix

HOTEL DES VOYAGEURS
Village centre
☎ (73) 71 11 76
Set in a little village in the Puy de Dôme, this 12-room *logis* serves good food in a pleasant dining room, and makes a point of welcoming visitors to the area. Well worth the stop. Menus from F55 to F90.

ll5100 St Flour

HOTEL ST JACQUES
6 Place Liberté
Ville Basse
☎ (71) 60 09 20
Another stop on my walk across France and a great welcome from all the staff. 28 rooms, a lift, and good menus in an elegant restaurant. Menus from F62 to F175. Recommended.

AUBERGE DE LA PROVIDENCE
1 Rue du Château d'Alleuze
☎ (71) 60 12 05
A small *auberge* with just 10 rooms and very good value menus ranging from F100 to F160.

48310 Fournels

HOTEL DU BES
Town centre
St Juéry
☎ (66) 31 61 82
A very small hotel on the frontier between Lozère and Cantal, which follows the course of the River Bés. No great gastronomic delights, but a delightful village, once the home of that awesome werewolf, the *Bête de Gévaudan*. Good fishing. Menus at F50 and F80. Highly recommended. Do visit the church here – the interior is magnificent.

63740 Gelles

HOSTELLERIE DU COMMERCE
Village centre
☎ (73) 87 80 01
Jean-Luc Monnet was the Auvergne regional champion in the 1987 *Logis de France* Cookery Contest with his *truite soufflée avec sa julienne de légumes*. Gelles is a quiet little town east of the Puy de Dôme, at no great distance from Orcival. Only five rooms, so the

restaurant is important, and it is best to book. Menus from F46 to F105.

15390 Loubaresse

HOTEL BEAU-SITE
Viaduct de Garabit
Garabit
☎ (71) 23 41 46
The spectacular railway viaduct built by Eiffel draws visitors to this spot, which boasts four *logis*. This one has the least rooms (16), but the best menus, priced from F82 to F150. Recommended.

43150 Le Monastier-sur-Gazeille

LE MOULIN DE SAVIN
Town centre
☎ (71) 03 80 89
Robert Louis Stevenson set out on his *Travels with a Donkey in the Cévennes* from this little town in the Vélay, hence the inclusion here of this 1-star *logis*. 10 rooms, menus from F50 to F110. Worth a visit.

43580 Monistrol d'Allier

HOTEL SARDA
Town centre
☎ (71) 57 21 96
Another good stop on the pilgrims' road west of Le Puy, run by an Anglo-French couple, the Wests. Good menus from F60 to F175, and a very warm welcome from the hosts. If you are going to Compostela from Le Puy, don't forget to sign their visitors' book, full of pilgrims' names.

15300 Murat

HOTEL DE LA SANTOIRE
Carrière de Ségur
☎ (71) 20 70 68
I stayed in this hotel in Cantal during my walk across France. It is actually at some distance from Murat, on the road towards Lioran, south of Condat. M. Chabrier is a keen walker and his pleasant hotel near the Monts de Cantal is an ideal base for walking, as well as serving excellent food. 30 rooms, good menus from F40 to F120. Highly recommended.

AUBERGE DU TUNNEL
Lioran
☎ (71) 49 50 02
I stayed in this little hotel by the tunnel under the Plomb de Cantal during my walk across France, and M. Lebas made me very welcome. Lioran is a ski resort and walking centre in picturesque country, well worth a visit. 18 rooms. Menus from F48 to F70. Recommended.

63790 Murol

LE BEAU SITE
Chambon-sur-Lac
☎ (73) 88 61 29
Set on a lake, a few miles from Murol, this hotel is set by the lake at Chambon, which occupies the crater of an extinct volcano and is a stunning sight under a blue summer sky. There are several hotels here but this one has good food and local dishes on menus from F60 to F120. 19 rooms.

RELAIS DES MONTAGNES
Beaune-le-Froid
☎ (73) 88 61 48
Little Beaune lies on a hill above Murol and the lake at Chambon. Murol has a great castle, well worth a diversion, but it is splendid walking country all the way to Besse. The *relais* has 12 rooms and inexpensive menus from F40 to F65.

63870 Orcines-La Baraque

HOTEL LE DOME
Summit of the Puy
☎ (73) 91 49 00
Ten people live on the top of this extinct volcano in the Parc de Volcans, most of them in this 2-star hotel, which has four rooms and menus from F87 to F175, plus terrific views. Not to be missed.

RELAIS DES PUYS
Village centre
☎ (73) 62 10 51
This hotel lies outside the village, on the D941. Quite large, with 28 rooms, it serves local dishes and has menus from F58 to F140. Closed Monday midday. Well worth a visit.

63210 Orcival

HOTEL NOTRE-DAME
Near the church
☎ (73) 65 82 02
Mme Daldin runs this cheerful little nine-room *logis* with the help of her son Nicolas. The hotel is just opposite the pilgrim church at Orcival and serves good food and an excellent St Porçain wine. Good value, with menus from F45 to F58. Restaurant closed Wednesday.

63380 Pontaumur

HOTEL DE LA POSTE
Ave du Marronnier
☎ (73) 79 90 15
This *logis*, in the wild country west of Clermont-Ferrand, is run with great efficiency and charm by Jean-Paul Quinty. The hotel is very new but the food is traditional. Try the *gratin du lotte*, or choose from menus priced between F50 and F160. 15 rooms.

43000 Le Puy

HOTEL DES VOYAGEURS
37 Boulevard Fayolle
☎ (71) 09 05 30
Le Puy is full of fine sights and well worth a visit for the cathedral alone. There are many good hotels, but this 15-room *logis* makes a point of including local dishes in its menus, which range from F58 to F100. Worth a visit.

63130 Royat

LA BELLE MEUNIERE
25 Ave de la Vallée
☎ (73) 35 80 17
Royat is a nice little town of the Puy-de-Dôme in the heart of the Auvergne, where M. Bon runs this excellent 2-star *logis*. 10 rooms. Good food on menus from F127 to F250. Excellent wine list.

143170 Saugues

HOTEL DE LA TERRASSE
Town centre
☎ (71) 77 83 10
A small 14-room hotel on the Road to Compostela, east of le Puy. Good reliable menus priced from F55 to F130. No gastronomic paradise, but excellent value.

RHONE VALLEY

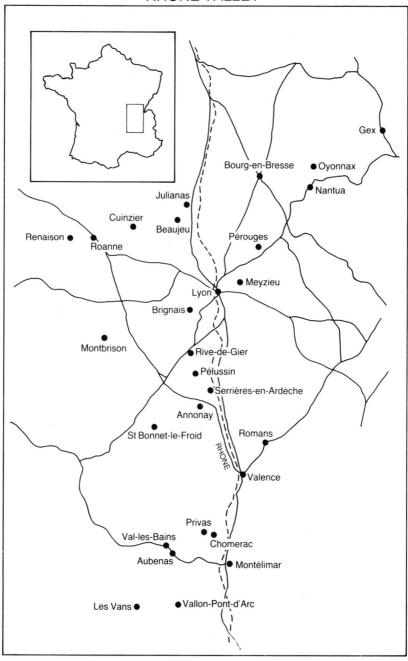

Gex

Bourg-en-Bresse   Oyonnax

Nantua

Julianas

Cuinzier   Beaujeu   Pérouges

Renaison   Roanne

Meyzieu

Lyon

Brignais

Montbrison   Rive-de-Gier

Pélussin

Serrières-en-Ardèche

Annonay

St Bonnet-le-Froid   Romans

RHONE

Valence

Privas

Val-les-Bains   Chomerac

Aubenas   Montélimar

Les Vans   Vallon-Pont-d'Arc

RHONE VALLEY

The Valley of the Rhône, that great river that flows out of Switzerland and then south into the Mediterranean at the Camargue delta, also travels through the gastronomic heart of France, which is said to beat most strongly in the city of Lyon at the junction of the Saône and the Rhône. If this is so, these rivers have made a considerable contribution to this gastronomic success, not only in providing certain products, such as fish, but in providing the means through which a wide variety of other products can reach this central part of France. The Rhône is surrounded by rich lands and gathers in the best they produce to enhance the skills of the local cuisine.

As in many other parts of France, the Rhône Valley is a modern creation, cobbled together from old provinces and dukedoms, with large sections of Burgundy attached to the northern end. The region comprises five *départements*: Loire, Rhône, and Ain in the north, and to the south the wild Ardèche and the mountainous Drôme. These rugged areas to the south are balanced by the gentle, lake-dotted country of the Ain, the wine hills of the Beaujolais north of Lyon, and by the urban attractions of several large provincial cities, Bourg-en-Bresse, Valence and most notably, the striking and attractive city of Lyon, which probably has more good restaurants than any single city of France, except Paris.

Access to the Rhône valley is easy. There is an excellent airport at Lyon (Satolas), 20 miles east of the city, the TGV express trains speed south from Paris in three hours or less, and the area is transfixed by the A7 autoroute and the N6 and N7 Routes Nationales. When suggesting a tour, it seems safe to assume that most English-speaking travellers will come in from the north-west and enter through the N7 at Roanne – already on most gastronomic lists as the home of the Trois-Gros, which, with three Michelin rosettes, is practically a place of pilgrimage for the dedicated gastronome. From here head east across the rolling vineyard-covered hills of the Beaujolais, to all those places which appear so often on the wine labels: Julianas, Moulin à Vent – where there *is* a windmill incidentally – and the little village of Vaux-en-Beaujolais, near the town of Villefranche, which is said to be the original Clochemerle, a claim supported by the fact that it contains the *Caves de Clochemerle* as the local *dégustation* centre. North of here lies Cluny, once a centre for the great monastic order, the Cluniacs, whose abbey was largely destroyed in the Revolution, and this Burgundian centre lies outside the new Rhône Valley area. To the east lies the country of Bresse, and the town of Bourg-en-Bresse, famous for its chickens and cheese. The great church at Brou, just to the east of the town, should not be missed either. Neither, for that matter, should the Auberge Bressane, another temple of gastronomy, just opposite the church.

The Ain, which lies south of Bresse, is flat farming country, full of small lakes, with a very large one providing a doormat for the town of Nantua, which lies at the foot of the Jura Massif. From here, turning in the direction of Lyon, the next significant stop is the tour of Pérouges, really a fortified village and full of beautiful fifteenth-century houses. Pérouges is often used as a centre for companies filming costume dramas, and although it is now something of a tourist trap, it is still well worth seeing. To the east of Pérouges lies Bellay, a small town in beautiful countryside but notable to gastronomes as the home of the famous writer Brillat-Savarin. Brillat-Savarin was also a judge, and did not finish his great treatise on gastronomy, *La Physiologie de la Goût* until he was 70. Only a Frenchman could think of a title like that.

Lyon is a fine city set at the confluence of the Rhône and the Saône, and worth weeks of time or several visits. It has scores of good restaurants, theatres, cinemas, parks and lots of small *quartiers*, those by the river linked by a network of alleyways known as *traboules*. Like Paris, Lyon would justify a book on its own, but since it is a provincial city, I have included it here and listed some of the restaurants, chosen from a wide selection.

East of Lyon, and with the snow-tipped mountains already in sight, the land rises slowly towards Grenoble and the Alps. There are many ski resorts further east in the Isère – Val d'Isère, for example – but Isère is an Alpine *département*. The Rhône flows south into the wine country again at Tournon and Valence and Romans. At Tournon the Côtes du Rhône vineyards begin, with those of Hermitage close by.

Valence was once a Roman town, part of that *Provincia Romana* which gave its name to Provence. Tournon actually lies in the Ardèche, but the greater part of that wildly beautiful *département*, the ancient Viverais, lies west of the river. The capital of the Ardèche is the little town of Privas, but the fact that this central town has a population of just 10,000 will indicate that the Ardèche is a country of small villages and narrow, winding roads, a place to wander in. The canoe journey down the Ardèche to Vallon-Pont de l'Arche is a famous trip, but on the way north do stop at Annonay, capital of the Haut-Viverais, and also set in superb country.

The River Loire rises in the Ardèche, on the slopes of the volcanic Gerbier de Jonc, and the Loire *département* to which it gives its name, lies to the north of Annonay and west of Lyon. Places to visit here include the town of Montbrison, the castle at La Bastie d'Urfe and although it is industrial, the city of St Etienne, which is most famous in France for its football team but also contains some notable restaurants.

In truth, this is a region to wander in, but if I had to choose I would opt for the Ardèche, the hills of the Forez west of Lyon, and the little golden villages of the Beaujolais – plus a day or two in Lyon, of course.

Essential sights

Lyon, a very fine city, with good restaurants and excellent shopping, so allow two days. Pérouges, a little gem, and for a surprise, a tour from here across to Ain to Nantua. Go south to see the Roman remains of old Provence at Valence and Tournon. Cruise about the Beaujolais country north-west of Lyon, buying a bottle here, a bottle there, and follow the *Route de Beaujolais*, which takes in the main wine villages. Try the canoe trip through the Gorges de l'Ardèche to Vallon-Pont de l'Arche. See the great church at Brou near Bourg-en-Bresse. Visit the area around Tournon for the Hermitage vineyards. Finally, wander into the hills of the Ardèche to find some of the most wild and least-visited country in France.

Food

Every good guide concurs with my view, and that of Curnousky, that this Rhône Valley area is one of the great gastronomic regions of France, most of them putting in a word for the formidable *mères* of Lyon, who by tradition dominate the restaurant kitchens of that fine city. This is unusual because the common practice in France is that the man does the cooking while his wife runs the restaurant and overawes the clientele. Typically local dishes can vary from the simple to the rich, with great use of the potato – *pommes Lyonnaise* – with potatoes and onions they are succulent examples. Lyon is also noted for *charcuterie*, and a range of solid fare, including *quenelles de brochet*, or pike mousse. Another local speciality, though often expensive, is *poulet demi-deuil*, chicken with truffles. *Friture* is fried whitebait from the Rhône. *Sauce Nantua* is made with crayfish, butter and cream. Any dish prepared *à la Lyonnaise* comes with onions. Bresse chickens, reared on corn, are of an attractive golden colour, and Bresse also has a famous cheese, the Bleu de Bresse. Other cheeses worth sampling are the Petit Bresson, a goat's milk cheese, as is the Cabrion de Forez, and a personal favourite, from cow's milk, the Rigotte de Condrieu. Picodon, from Montélimar, is the only local goat's cheese.

Wine

Although it is not considered one of the *great* wine areas of France, the Rhône Valley contains a great deal of excellent wine from Mâcon, Beaujolais and, above all, the Côtes-du-Rhône. Not all Beaujolais is *nouveau*, although those who like their red wine at room temperature may avoid dramas if they know that in the Beaujolais especially, it is common to drink red wine chilled. I was in a restaurant in Julianas when an Englishman made a dreadful scene on this issue, bellowing 'Chambré! Chambré!' at the alarmed patron. The memory is with me still. In the Beaujolais, try the local wines from the villages, Julianas, Moulin à Vent, Brouilly, Morgan, and so on, which are usually several grades above mere plonk. Further south there are the wines of the Côtes-du-Rhône, and from the Côte-Rotie comes Hermitage. To this one can add the less notable wines of Crozes-Hermitage, the fruity Condrieu, and from the Ardèche, Cornas, a very substantial red. Do not neglect the lesser-known vintages, such as the light, fruity Côtes du Forez or the Rousette de Vivieu from Bresse, or the wines from the Bugay in the Ain, where the whites of Cerdon are very good. The wines hereabouts tend to be red, but those who would like to sample a local sparkling white can try the St Péray or the good wines of Mâcon.

RESTAURANTS

07100 Annonay

CHEZ MARC ET CHRISTINE
Opposite the station
☎ (75) 33 46 97
A good, central, family-run restaurant in the centre of this little Ardeçois town. Menus from F95 to F235. Closed Sunday evening and Monday.

HOTEL DU MIDI
17 Place des Cordeliers
☎ (75) 33 23 77
A large *logis* for the Ardèche, with 20 rooms. A good centre for touring the wild country around this little town. No restaurant but good food available from Chez Marc et Christine, and other restaurants in the town.

07200 Aubenas

RESTAURANT LE FOURNIE
34 Rue de 4 Septembre
Place Olivier de Sèvres
☎ (75) 93 58 68
This is a cellar restaurant tucked away in a maze of narrow streets off the central square. Menus from F80, with very good food, including local specialities. Try the *flan de chataigne couli de fraises*, a real triumph of a dessert.

AUBERGE PONSON
Quartier Ponson
☎ (75) 35 07 78
A pleasant little *logis* in the wild and beautiful Ardèche, with 12 rooms and good, inexpensive food on menus priced from F55 to F75. Restaurant closed Sunday.

69430 Beaujeu

HOTEL ANNE DE BEAUJEU
28 Rue République
☎ (74) 04 87 58
A little seven-room *logis* with very good menus ranging from F95 to F250. This *logis* concentrates on offering local wines and good local food. Highly recommended.

01300 Bellay

HOTEL DU BUGEY
10 Rue Georges Girerd
☎ (79) 91 01 46
The wines of Bugey deserve to be better known, and a good range of local vintages can be sampled here at this welcoming 12-room *logis*. Menus from F52 to F150. Excellent value. Recommended.

43290 St Bonnet-le-Froid

AUBERGE DES CIMES
Montfaucon
☎ (71) 59 93 72
This little village is actually on the Ardèche-Haute Loire border, but why haggle? This small hotel, with just seven rooms, serves the most splendid dishes, even on the F90 menu – *cuisse de canard confit des herbes*, for example. The other menus are equally fine, with the F200 one a positive feast. Good wine list. Highly recommended.

01000 Bourg-en-Bresse

AUBERGE BRESSANE
166 Boulevard de Brou
☎ (74) 22 22 68
One of the great restaurants of the area, situated just opposite the marvellous church of Brou. Can be crowded, so it is best to book, but excellent value, with menus from F161 to F368. Recommended for that special meal.

69530 Brignais

RESTOTEL
Les Aigais
Route de Lyon
☎ (78) 05 24 57
Brignais is a medieval town, with just this one 30-room *logis*, where the restaurant serves good food on menus ranging from F90 to F220.

07210 Chomerac

RESTAURANT LOUIS ESCLOS
Alissas
☎ (75) 65 12 73
This little restaurant is 2 miles outside Privas on the road to Montélimar. Menus from F80 to F120.

42460 Cuinzier

HOTEL BEL 'VUE
Le Cergne
☎ (74) 89 77 56
Another small *logis* of the Loire *département*. Just eight rooms but a first-class restaurant serving *tourte saumon*; *rognons de veau bourbonnais* and other excellent dishes on menus from F70 to F240. Recommended.

01170 Gex

HOTEL DU PARC
Town centre
☎ (50) 41 50 18
A small village in the Ain, with just this one good *logis*. 19 rooms and excellent food on menus from F110 to F270. Recommended.

69840 Julianas

CHEZ LA ROSE
Place du Marché
☎ (74) 04 41 20
A beautiful little village of the Beaujolais, with two *logis*. This one has 12 rooms, menus from F60 to F150, local dishes and, of course, local wines.

69001 Lyon

MERE BRAZIER
12 Rue Royale
☎ (78) 28 15 49
Lyon is full of good restaurants, but this typically Lyonnaise establishment can stand for all the rest. It is one of those with a Michelin rosette, serves local food like *quenelles au gratin*, and is far from formal. I like it. Menus from F230 to F285. Worth every centime.

69330 Meyzieu

LE MONT JOYEUX
Ave Victor Hugo
☎ (78) 04 21 32
Well off the too-well-beaten track, this rather smart *logis* has a very good wine list and well-chosen menus from F80 to F200. 20 rooms. Restaurant closed Sunday evening and Monday.

42600 Montbrison

HOTEL DES VOYAGEURS
16 Rue St Boyer
☎ (77) 96 17 64
Montbrison is a pleasant town, a good centre for the hills of the Forez.
This 11-room *logis*, one of two in the town, has one good F68 menu –
excellent value. Restaurant closed Saturday evening and Sunday.

26200 Montélimar

LE MISTRAL
Route Nationale 7
Châteauneuf-du-Rhône
☎ (75) 01 22 42
Just seven rooms, so the restaurant is the main business of this 2-star
logis. Menus from F60 to F120.

HOTEL DU PRINTEMPS
8 Chemin de la Manche
☎ (75) 01 32 63
Montélimar, best known for the manufacture of nougat, has several
excellent hotels and restaurants. Good Rhône wines and well-chosen
dishes on menus priced from F85 to F220. Restaurant closed Sunday
outside high season.

01130 Nantua

HOTEL DE LYON
19 Rue de Docteur Mercier
☎ (74) 75 17 09
Nantua is a beautiful little lakeside town of the Ain, well worth a
visit. Stay and/or eat at this nice little 18-room *logis*. Menus from F85
to F200. Try the fish, and the wines of Bugey.

01100 Oyonnax

CHEZ BUFFARD
Place de l'Eglise
☎ (74) 77 86 01
An attractive corner of the Ain can be explored from this pleasant
country town. This *logis* has 28 rooms and the restaurant has well-
chosen menus that range from F99 to F250.

42410 Pélussin

HOTEL DE L'ANCIENNE GARE
Village centre
☎ (74) 87 61 51
Pélussin is a good centre for the hills and forests of the Forez, east of Lyon. This hotel, just seven rooms and the smallest of three *logis* in the town, won the *Logis de France* Cookery Contest with menus which include dishes such as *foie gras sur toast, saumon au beurre fine* and *truite Limousine*. Menus from F50 to F170. Highly recommended.

01800 Pérouges

HOSTELLERIE DU VIEUX PEROUGES
Town centre
☎ (74) 61 00 88
Pérouges is a beautiful place, and even if a tourist trap it should not be missed on a tour of the Ain. This old *logis* serves good food on menus priced from F160 to F360.

07000 Privas

AUBERGE LION D'OR
29 Rue de la République
☎ (75) 64 11 43
A good, small *logis*, with 10 inexpensive rooms and menus to match, from F42 to F110. Restaurant closed Saturday night and Sunday night.

42370 Renaison

HOTEL-RESTAURANT JACQUES COEUR
15 Rue de Roanne
☎ (77) 64 25 34
The beautiful dining room and the excellent dishes, such as *Emince de boeuf Côte Roannaise*, draw guests and diners to this attractive 10-room *logis* at the foot of the Côte Roannaise. Menus from F70 to F240, offering a wide choice of regional dishes.

42800 Rive-de-Gier

HOTEL LA PRIEURE
Ste Croix-en-Jarez
☎ (77) 20 20 09
A small hotel, 5 miles from Rive-de-Gier, between Lyon and St Etienne. Only three rooms, but a good big restaurant in a beautiful ancient hotel. Excellent menus from F75 to F200.

42300 Roanne

AUBERGE CASTELLOISE
2 Ave Libération
☎ (77) 68 12 71
People flock to Roanne to eat at the Trois-Gros with its three Michelin rosettes, but you can also eat marvellously well at this pleasant one-rosette restaurant. Menus from F160 to F235. Recommended.

26100 Romans

AUBERGE PONTON
40 Place Jacquemart
☎ (75) 02 29 91
A very small *logis*, with just three rooms, but what a restaurant! Menus from F98 to F200, the latter with a huge selection of dishes. Highly recommended when passing through the Drôme. Restaurant closed Sunday evening and Thursday.

07340 Serrières-en-Ardèche

HOTEL SCHAEFFER
Route Nationale 86
☎ (75) 34 00 07
Serrières is a pleasant little town on the Rhône east of Annonay. This modern hotel is very comfortable, a good night-stop on the way north, with good food matched by Côtes-du-Rhône wines in the dining room. 12 rooms. Menus from F125 to F250, so good-quality meals may be expected. Restaurant closed Monday evening and Tuesday.

07300 Tain-Tournon

HOTEL LA CHAUMIERE
76 Quai Farconet
☎ (75) 08 07 78
Only 10 rooms but very good food in the restaurant of this attractive *logis* by the Rhône. Menus range in price from F80 to F185. Recommended, not least for the excellent range of Côtes-du-Rhône wines.

RESTAURANT REYNAUD
82 Ave Président Roosevelt
☎ (75) 07 22 10
Perhaps the best of the local restaurants, this has excellent food and a great range of Hermitage and Côtes-du-Rhône wines. Menus from F120 to F260. Recommended.

26000 Valence

LA LICORNE
13 Rue Henri Chalamet
☎ (75) 43 76 83
A very good restaurant in a town full of good restaurants. The menus are priced from F60 to F130 – excellent value. Try the *coquilles St-Jacques*, and the cheeseboard with one of the local wines. Highly recommended.

07600 Val-les-Bains

HOTEL L'EUROPE
86 Rue Jean-Jaurès
☎ (75) 37 43 94
A pleasant hotel with 35 inexpensive rooms and a good country restaurant with menus from F80 to F150. The F105 menu has such dishes as *saumon frais meunière Nantais*, and *moules au saffron*. Good selection of cheeses and fine wine list. Recommended.

07150 Vallon-Pont-d'Arc

LE BELVEDERE
Opposite the 'Arc'
☎ (75) 88 00 02
This little town draws in visitors to see the famous natural rock arch over the river. This *logis*, with 16 rooms, is one of four in the town but is the one serving local food. Menus from F60 to F110.

07140 Les Vans

CHATEAU LE SCIPIONNET
Route de Joyeuse
☎ (75) 37 23 84
A small château hotel with 13 rooms and a good terrace restaurant, serving good food and grills at prices from F110.

THE ALPS: SAVOIE-DAUPHINE

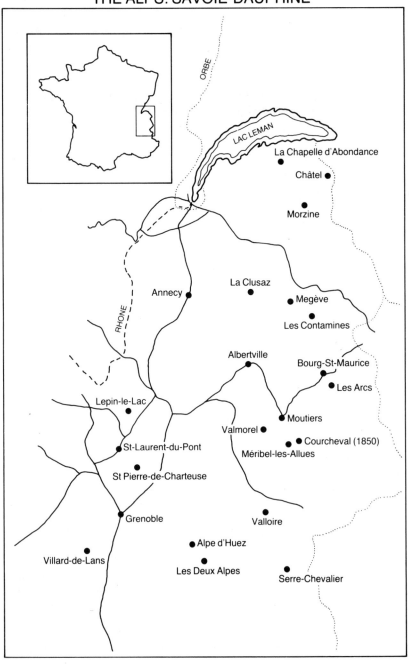

THE ALPS
SAVOIE-DAUPHINE

The French Alps, which run down the eastern side of France from Lac Leman (Lake Geneva) to the doorstep of the Mediterranean, are best known to Europe's travellers as a ski area. From Christmas to Easter, weather permitting, these mountains are deep in snow and criss-crossed with ski trails, but the mountains of Savoie and the Dauphiné also have another existence and are equally popular in summer with legions of walkers and climbers, who flock to Chamonix or one of several National Parks, to scale the local peaks or walk in some of the most beautiful and spectacular mountain scenery on Earth.

This region falls broadly into two parts, Savoie and Haute-Savoie, which were once part of the Italian kingdom of Savoy, and the Dauphiné, which, from 1349 until the Revolution, provided a rather thin living for the eldest son of the King of France, the Dauphin. The modern Alps-Savoie-Dauphiné region comprises just four *départements* – Savoie and Haute-Savoie and, in the Dauphiné, Isère and Hautes-Alpes. These *départements* are less well-known than some of the places they contain, Courcheval, Val d'Isère, Chamonix, Morzane, Avoriaz, Flaine, Les Deux-Alpes, Megève, and since most of my readers will visit this region to stay and ski in a local ski resort, getting about may not be so important. Ski resorts apart though, this region contains some many very fine towns and beautiful old villages, such as Annecy, Grenoble, Aime, and Chartreuse. Those who have seen it in winter should return in the summer.

Moreover, the summer visitors do have much easier access. They will probably come in either through Geneva, that great entrepôt for skiers or, if heading for the Dauphiné, through the airport at Lyon-Satolas, and then along the A48 or A41 autoroutes to Grenoble. To begin in the north, the first leg of any tour through the French Alps is usually along the Lac d'Annecy, past Annecy itself and up to such places as Megève, Flaine or the many ski resorts of the Portes du Soleil. Further south lies the Tarentaise area, where Tignes, Val d'Isère and La Plagne are famous names. Courcheval is the prettiest resort of the Trois Vallées, and since this is the most French, it also has the best restaurants. Then comes the glacier-filled Parc des Ecrins and its larger neighbour, the Parc de Vanoise, both marvellous places for walking and hill-trekking, and then the walled town of Briançon, fortified for Louis XIV by Vauban. There is another small clutch of ski resorts near here, Puy St Vincent, Risoul, Montgénevre, but all ski resorts are developing a summer trade, so the hotels are open in the June–September period as well as during the winter season. Most of these resorts are fairly modern and therefore functional rather than pretty, especially if seen without a mantle of snow.

South of here lies the fine town of Gap, capital of the Hautes-Alpes, a main stop on the Route Napoléon, which the Emperor followed during the Hundred Days before Waterloo, after he returned from exile on Elba. The Route Napoléon can be followed north to the city of Grenoble, a city of parks and museums, and a large university. Grenoble lies at the foot of the Vercors plateau, a beautiful high mountain area, with Villard-de-Lans and Lans as the main holiday centres. The Alps make a marvellous background for a car touring holiday, but to enjoy this region to the full you must either walk or ski.

Essential sights

Drive through or walk in the glacier-filled Parc des Ecrins, or the gloriously empty spaces of the Parc de Vanoise. Visit the spa town of Evian on Lac Leman, and the old parts of Annecy. A lake cruise from either place is a great experience. Grenoble is a very fine town, quite lively, as a university town tends to be, and from here it is no distance up to the Vercors.

The Chartreuse monastery, founded in 1101, is well worth a visit, both for the liqueur, which is still made there, and for the surrounding scenery. Briançon has Vauban walls. Chamonix is the great centre for alpinists, and cable cars run up to the heights as well as a train to the Mer de Glace below Mont Blanc, at 15,770 ft (4807 m), the highest mountain in Europe. Chambery is a centre for the vineyards of Apremont.

Food

The food of the Alps tends to reflect the environment and history. Fondues, either cheese or meat, are very popular, although I once enjoyed a dozen succulent oysters, served on a bed of snow, during a winter visit to Val d'Isère. There is good mountain ham, locally caught trout, and local specialities such as *pommes Dauphinois* and fondue Savoyard. Any combinations of potatoes and cheese, topped with breadcrumbs, are called *gratins*. The cheeses are very good, with Beaufort, the many-holed, the pungent Roblochon, Comte and the little Tomme cheeses of Savoie being especially excellent, but look out also for the Bleu de Tignes. Grenoble is famous for walnuts. Other dishes, usually of the rib-sticking variety, include *omelette Savoyarde*, which comes filled with fried potatoes and cheese; *gratin Dauphinoise*, potatoes cooked in milk, with grated nutmeg and cheese – delicious – and *soupe Montagnarde*, a vegetable soup with a crust of grated cheese. Veal, ham, cheese, fish from the mountain streams, and good stews make up the mainstream of Alpine cuisine.

Wine

Some very drinkable local wines come from the vineyards of Savoie, most of it white, dry and sparkling, or at least *pétillant*. The main wines of Savoie are from Apremont or Ayse, which has a good sparkling white, but there is also the very good Rousette de Savoie, and many wines from the Arbois. Other wines to look out for are the whites of Crépy, which are *pétillant*, with small bubbles, and the scented wine from Seyssel, which goes well with a cheese fondue. The best reds of the AC Vins de Savoie come from Chautagne and Montmélian. As a *vin de pays*, try the Dalmes Dauphinoises. None of this wine is remarkable, but it all goes well with the local food. Don't forget the green or yellow liqueur from Chartreuse, or the local Evian water.

RESTAURANTS

73200 Albertville

LE LIGISMOND
Cité-Médiéval de Conflans
☎ (79) 32 53 50
Most skiers know Albertville as a grubby town between Geneva and the slopes. In the old *cité* of Conflans you can discover this very agreeable restaurant with good menus from F95 to F295.

38750 Alpe d'Huez

AU CHAMOIS D'OR
Route de Fontbelle
☎ (76) 80 31 32
Said to be the best restaurant in this pre-war-established ski resort, and the food on my infrequent visits seems to bear this out. Good views over the *pistes*, menus from F105 to F135, plus *carte*. Good wine list.

74000 Annecy

LA CIBOULETTE
10 Rue Vaugelas
☎ (50) 45 74 57
M. Paccard has run this excellent restaurant to the great satisfaction of the locals for many years, and it will repay a visit. Excellent, soundly prepared dishes with menus from F105 to F135, and *carte*. Good, short wine list. Highly recommended.

73700 Les Arcs

RESTAURANT LE GREEN
Arc 1800
☎ (79) 07 25 17
This restaurant gives a marvellous view of Mont Blanc and serves good food, much better than standard Alpine fare, with menus from F250 to F300. The place for that big night out or the (very) long lunch.

73700 Bourg-St-Maurice

HOTEL LE CONCORDE
Ave Maréchal Leclerc
☎ (79) 07 08 90
A good 32-room *logis*, with a restaurant serving Savoyard fare (not just *raclette*). Menus from F70 to F100.

74360 La Chapelle d'Abondance

LES CORNETTES DE BISES
Village centre
☎ (50) 73 50 24
A larger *logis* with 40 rooms and menus ranging widely from F80 to F300. I fancy you will eat very well anywhere in La Chapelle d'Abondance, because I am told that the restaurants in this Alpine village compete for the custom of visitors and there is considerable rivalry between the chefs.

HOTEL L'ENSOLEILLE
Village centre
☎ (50) 73 50 42
A friend who knows the area well confirms that the restaurants of La Chapelle vie with each other to produce ever-better food. This one, with 34 rooms, has menus from F70 to F220.

LE VIEUX MOULIN
Route de Chevennes
☎ (50) 73 52 52
With only 16 rooms, which may be a good sign, this *logis* offers regional dishes on menus priced from F70 to F200. A good range of prices and an excellent chef make for first-class value.

74390 Châtel

LE KANDAHAR
Clos du Tour
☎ (50) 73 30 60
A 10-room *logis* in this small Savoyard village, with good local food and generous menus from F65 to F150. Recommended.

74220 La Clusaz

HOTEL LE BELLACHAT
Les Confins
☎ (50) 02 40 50
A fair-sized *logis* with 25 rooms, and superior menus priced from F70

to F170. There are six *logis* in La Clusaz, but this is probably the best for food.

LE VIEUX CHALET
Les Tollets
☎ (50) 02 41 53
Half a mile from La Clusaz, this little restaurant has always been popular with the locals. Short, well-chosen menus priced from F72 to F190. Recommended.

73120 Courcheval (1850 metres)
LE CABICHOU
Quartier Les Chenus
☎ (79) 08 00 55
Courcheval is the rather smart ski resort of the Trois Vallées, and this hotel-restaurant attracts the French in droves. Not cheap, with the *carte* costing about F500, but excellent food on menus from F220 to F450. Recommended.

74920 Conbloux

CHALET-HOTEL LE FEUG
Conbloux
☎ (50) 193 00 50
This hotel-restaurant, 1½ miles from the centre of Megève, is a great skiing hotel, looking out on Mont Blanc. Good menus in a sunny restaurant.

HOTEL IDEAL MONT-BLANC
Route du Feu
☎ (50) 58 60 54
This is the hotel with the reputation for good local food. 25 rooms and varied menus from F115 to F150. Recommended.

74190 Les Contamines

HOTEL LE MIAGE
☎ (50) 47 01 63
A small 11-room *logis* and a good lunchtime stop, with menus from F80 to F250. Recommended.

LE TETRAS PUB
Les Hameaux du Lay
☎ (50) 47 08 49
The Tétras is an English-style pub in this popular ski resort of the Montjoie valley, run by Patrick Deschodt, who speaks English and

caters specifically for British skiers and walkers. Not *haute cuisine* but sausages, soups, pancakes . . . even Welsh rarebit. Good fun.

38860 Les Deux Alpes

LES MARMOTTES
Village centre
☎ (76) 79 21 91
Reliable, traditional food is the hallmark of this agreeable restaurant in the equally agreeable ski resort of Les Deux Alpes. Menus from F125 to F175. *Carte* from F250. Good wine list.

38000 Grenoble

A MA TABLE
92 Cours Jean-Jaurès
☎ (76) 96 77 04
Another nice little restaurant, popular with local people, which visitors should seek out. Good wines, cheerful, friendly staff, and excellent food. *Carte* only, from F200 to F250. Recommended.

38380 St-Laurent-du-Pont

HOTEL LES TROIS BICHES
Miribel-Les-Echelles
☎ (76) 55 28 02
A tiny *logis* in this village of the Isère, with just six rooms, but M. Comba won the *Logis de France* Regional Cookery Competition with his *escalope de saumon, pochée au coules de poireaux.* Menus from F50 to F120.

73610 Lepin-le-Lac

LE CLOS SAVOYARD
Lac d'Aiguebelette
☎ (79) 36 00 15
A 15-room *logis*, off the beaten track, where the restaurant serves Savoyard dishes on menus from F85 to F200. A very good summer spot for mountain walkers.

74120 Megève

AUBERGE LES GRIOTTES
Route de Megève
☎ (50) 21 24 43
Mostly fish, ideal for weightwatchers, the *crème* of *le Tout Paris*, who

flock here. A friendly welcome and bearable prices. Menus from F65 to F140. Recommended.

CHEZ NINO'S
Rue d'Arly
☎ (50) 21 02 18
This is the great restaurant of Megève, and, for those who can afford it, worth every centime. Essential to book. No *raclette* or menus, except for lunch. Otherwise it's all *à la carte*. Expect to pay F300 to F400 per head.

HOTEL LES SAPINS
Route de Rochebrune
☎ (50) 21 02 79
Megève is popular with the glitterati of Paris and therefore can be expensive. But there is value for money at this 19-room roadside *logis*, and good food on menus priced from F117 to F180.

73550 Méribel-les-Allues

L'ESTANQUET
Résidence La Tougnette
☎ (79) 08 64 25
Méribel has many good restaurants, littered about the resort, but this is among the best, although some of the dishes are a little elaborate. Menus from F130 to F220. *Carte* about F250. Recommended.

74110 Morzine

LA CHAMADE
Town centre
(50) 79 13 91
La Chamade is the great restaurant of Morzine, below the resort of Avoriaz, and worth coming down for. Not cheap, with the only menu at F167, and expect to pay F300 to F350 for the *carte*.

73600 Moutiers

HOTEL LES ROCHES BRUNES
403 Faubourg de la Madeleine
☎ (79) 24 20 67
A small 15-room *logis* with a good restaurant offering local dishes on menus priced from F55 to F85. Excellent value.

38380 St Pierre-de-Chartreuse

AUBERGE L'ATRE FLEURIE
Route du Col de Porte (Route 512)
☎ (76) 88 60 21
A small eight-room *logis* that relies on the reputation of the restaurant, which serves excellent food and local dishes on menus from F50 to F170.

CHALET-HOTEL DU CUCHERON
☎ (76) 88 62 06
This 10-room hotel at the top of the Col du Cucheron is a popular spot with walkers and motorists. Menus from F64 to F125. Closed Tuesday. Recommended.

Le Praz (Courcheval 1350)

LE BISTRO DU PRAZ
Village centre
☎ (79) 08 10 52
Charlie's Bistro du Praz is one of the best lunchtime stops in the Trois Vallées, but not cheap – expect to pay F250 to F300 per head for excellent meals, with *foie gras*, *magret*, good soups and stews, *fondue des fruits de mer* (the shot of firewater from Charlie's private bottle comes free). Highly recommended.

05240 Serre-Chevalier

LA BOULE DE NEIGE
15 Rue du Centre
Chantemerle
☎ (92) 24 00 16
Just to be different, this restaurant has only menus, no *carte*, but the dishes are excellent and the portions generous. A pretty restaurant in a good ski resort. Menus from F80 to F150.

73450 Valloire

HOTEL LA SETAZ
Restaurant Le Gastilleur
Village centre
☎ (79) 59 01 03
Valloire is a popular ski resort, full of good *logis*, several serving local dishes. 22 rooms. This one has menus from F78 to F130 and a good wine list.

73260 Valmorel

AU PETIT SAVOYARD
☎ (79) 09 81 64
This is a very lively town-centre restaurant with all the traditional Savoyard dishes – the *raclette*, the *fondues*, the meals that go to the hips. Very cheery owner. Menus from F57 to F68 – not expensive. *Carte* from around F200.

38250 Villard-de-Lans

LE PRE FLEURI
☎ (76) 95 10 96
The Vercors plateau is a beautiful spot and Villard is a good touring centre. This 18-room *logis* has menus priced from F80 to F155.

AQUITAINE

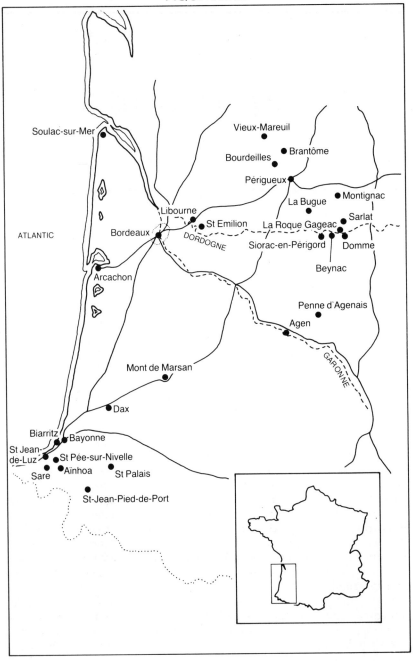

AQUITAINE

Modern Aquitaine, a large region which occupies much of western France south of the Gironde, stretching east up the Dordogne and the Garonne and deep south into the western Pyrenees, is nevertheless much smaller than the medieval Plantagenet Duchy. It now embraces the *départements* of Gironde, Dordogne, Lot-et-Garonne, Landes, and the country of the Basques, Pyrénées-Atlantiques. This is a vast and varied region, ideal for car touring, but the main centres are fairly compact and almost every *département* has something special to offer the visitor or those who come to build summer homes in the area.

In the Gironde lies the wine country of Bordeaux, where famous châteaux lie on every hand. Upriver in the Dordogne there is good wine at St Emilion, and then a procession of delights as the river leads the traveller further upstream. Essential visits on the way east are to the castle of Michel de Montaigne, the essayist, and the battlefield at Castillon, where in 1453 the English were finally defeated at the end of the Hundred Years War. Further upstream lies Bergerac, a centre for the wines of Duras and Montbazillac, as well as its own powerful reds, but also a tobacco centre. North of these lies Périgueux, capital of the Dordogne *département*, and a very fine town, but to the north of that there are two very pretty places, Brantôme and Bourdailles.

From Périgueux, move east to the Vézère and Terrasson-la-Villedieu, and visit the site of Lascaux, famous for prehistoric cave paintings, and the reconstruction at Lascaux II near Montignac, before following the Vézère down to the Dordogne near the great sweep of the Cingle de Trémolat. There are more prehistoric places here, at Les Eyzies, but then cross the river and take a tour through the *'bastide* country' and visit the small walled towns of Beaumont, Montpazier, Villefranche, with the castles of Belves, Biron – quite magnificent – leading you up to mighty Beynac and Fayrac, back on the river. Then comes little golden Domme, pitched high above the river and the fine town of Sarlat-en-Périgord, the most beautiful and evocative medieval town. One could spend years in the Dordogne and I know many people who return there summer after summer, but there is much more to Aquitaine than this one *département*.

South of Bordeaux, along the coast of the Landes, a region of sand-dunes and pine forests, you will find the port of Arcachon, and if you follow the coast south, you will arrive in the green country of the Basques. Bayonne is a very Basque city, and from there it is easy to visit the Edwardian splendours of Biarritz, and such pretty ports as St-Jean-de-Luz and the border town of Hendaye. The Basque country extends across the Pyrenees, but while Basque is spoken here and produces baffling roadsigns, the mountains of the western Pyrenees are green and very beautiful. Be sure to visit some of the Basque villages below the peak of La Rhune, places such as Aïnhoa and Cambo-les-Bains, Hasparren, St Palais and the little fortress town on the old Road to Compostela, St-Jean-Pied-de-Port.

North of the Pays Basque lies the county of Béarn, and the fine town of Pau, where Henry of Navarre was born. There are marvellous views of the Pyrenees from the esplanade at Pau, and from here you can drive south, deep into the mountains, to Arette and the Bigorre, before turning north for the Agenais.

Agen is a quaint little town and there are lots of good places to see in the surrounding Agenais, such as Villeneuve-sur-Lot, a large *bastide* town, or Nérac, on the River Garonne, before turning to Marmande and Cadillac and so, eventually, back to the splendid city of Bordeaux.

Essential sights

Allow at least a full day in Bordeaux, a very fine provincial city, and another day for touring and tasting in the vineyards of the Médoc, or the Entre-deux-Mers, the country between the Garonne and the Dordogne. Visit Libourne, the château of Montaigne, the castles at Biron and Beynac, the Vézère valley and the *bastides* at Montpazier and Domme. The classic sights of the Dordogne are the castle at Montfort and the town of Sarlat. Arcachon has excellent seafood and there are red squirrels in the forests of the Landes. Take the train up to the top of La Rhune in the Pays Basque, see a game of *pelota*, and

*Romanesque church at
Sauveterre-de-Béarn in
Pyrénées-Atlantiques*

A view of Annecy, in the Savoie-Dauphiné region

The fortified bridge at Orthez in Aquitaine

The Basque village of St-Jean-Pied-de-Port on the old Road to Compostela, in Aquitaine

A view of the bastide *of Villéreal in the Dordogne*

Estaing, one of the most beautiful places in the Lot valley

On the Cerdagne plateau in the Languedoc-Roussillon region

A villa in Corsica

visit St-Jean-Pied-de-Port, Cambo-les-Bains, Aïnhoa and Bayonne. Turning north, visit Pau and then cross the edge of the Armagnac country to Agen, heading west from there via Cadillac.

Food

The country of Aquitaine offers very good eating, from the Bordelais, the Périgord, the Pays Basque and the Landes – the choice is vast, the quality of produce excellent, the chefs experienced. The oysters of Arcachon are excellent, there is good seafood and tuna (*thon*) at St-Jean-de-Luz. I recommend *jambon pipérade*, ham with scrambled eggs and peppers, at St-Jean-Pied-de-Port, salmon from Navarrenx in the Pays Basque, the *poule au pot* of Pau, almost anything with *sauce bordelaise*. Food served *à la bordelaise* means with a red wine sauce. Try the truffles and goose and *foie gras* of the Périgord, the *cèpes* of Bordeaux, the prunes of Agen. Other local dishes worth looking out for include *poulet à la Basquaise* (chicken with ham and mushrooms), *coq au vin* (chicken in red wine), *sauté d'oie* (goose in a casserole), *confit de canard* (duck pâté), ham from Bayonne, guinea fowl and turkey (*dinde*) from the Landes. Bordeaux is the gastronomic centre of the region, but one can eat well almost everywhere. To the prepared dishes can be added marvellous fruit and vegetables and a great choice of wine.

Wine

There is so much wine in Aquitaine that it is hard to know where to start. The classic wines, the clarets so beloved of the English, come from the vineyards around Bordeaux, and vineyard visiting must take up some of the time during any visit to this area, which produces about half a billion bottles of AC wine every year! The major areas are Médoc, Graves and St Emilion, and the most prestigious chateaux are those of Margaux, Château-Lafite, Paulliac. Consult Don Phillpot's excellent guide, *The Vineyards of France*, for details of the wines and vineyards to visit. The local *vignerons* say that a good vineyard should 'see the river', and be laid out on one of the facing slopes. Wines to look out for are the sweet Sauternes and Barsac, the dry reds and whites from Graves, and moving up the Dordogne, those from St Emilion and Pomerol, fuller-bodied than the clarets of Bordeaux. Local wines much less expensive than the classic ones, are from the Côtes de Blaye, the Côtes de Bourg, the Côtes de Castillon, Bergerac, Duras, and for a sweet dessert wine, Montbazillac.

Sweet and dry whites come from the Entre-deux-Mers, and in the Landes there are local reds from Tarsan, and in the Pays Basque and the Pyrenees there are good wines from Juraçon and Madiran, while the Lot-et-Garonne and the Agenais offer good inexpensive wine from Buzet, the Côtes de Marmandais, and the *vin de pays Agenais*. There is wine here at all prices and of every quality, so drink the best you can afford.

RESTAURANTS

47450 Agen

LA CORNE D'OR
Colayrac-St-Cirq
☎ (53) 47 02 76
This 3-star *logis*, in a small village north-west of Agen, has 14 rooms and good menus priced from F100 to F200. Closed Saturday and Sunday evening.

64790 Aïnhoa

HOTEL OHANTZEA
Village centre
☎ (59) 29 90 50
The name of the hotel and its owner – M. Ithurria, are just two indications that this is the Pays Basque, and the food, with lots of spices and peppers, also reflects this fact. 10 rooms, cheerful staff and good menus from F90 to F180. Restaurant closed Sunday evening and Tuesday lunchtime. Aïnhoa is a beautiful Basque village, set in spectacular country.

33120 Arcachon

LA DUCHESSE ANNE
Front de Mer
☎ (56) 83 70 33
Arcachon was a fishing port before the tourists moved in and you will dine very well here on *fruits de mer*, fish, *magrets de canard, foie gras*. Terrace restaurant, very bracing.

64100 Bayonne

LA BELUGA
15 Rue des Tonneliers
☎ (59) 25 52 13
Bayonne is a very fine, very Basque town, full of life and good

restaurants. The Beluga majors on fish, with *son haddock, son beau turbot* and *magnifiques coquilles St-Jacques*, to name but a few dishes. *Carte* only, about F250 without wine.

24220 Beynac

HOTEL BONNET
Cazenac-St-Cyprian
☎ (53) 29 50 01
Beynac has a mighty castle, glowering across the green Dordogne valley towards Feyrac and Domme. This riverside *logis* has 22 rooms and a terraced restaurant with good dishes on menus priced from F90 to F175. Recommended.

HOTEL PONTET
Restaurant Maleville
☎ (53) 29 50 06
This fine hotel-restaurant is just by the river, with great views across to Feyrac if you sit facing upstream. A first-floor restaurant with willows just outside the terrace. Popular with the locals. Menus from F80 to F200. Recommended.

64200 Biarritz

LE GALION
17 Boulevard de Général de Gaulle
☎ (59) 24 20 32
In a fine Edwardian-style town like Biarritz it would be a crime to stint on the food. So dine here, not over-expensively, at Michel Barbe's excellent restaurant. Varied food, not all fish – sound dishes, *carte* only. Expect to pay F250 to F300 a head with wine.

33000 Bordeaux

LE CHAPON FIN
5 Rue Montesquieu
☎ (56) 79 10 10
Bordeaux has scores of excellent restaurants, but few match and none excel the Chapon Fin. Not cheap, certainly, with menus starting at F200 and rising to F350 or more, without wine, but if time and pocket allow, this is the place to choose. Highly recommended.

BISTRO DU CLAVEL
Gare St Jean
44 Rue Charles Domercq
☎ (56) 92 91 52

Less elaborate and much easier on the pocket than the above restaurant is this pleasant bistro in the centre of the town. Menus from F130 to F160. Good wine list.

24310 Bourdeilles

HOTEL GRIFFONS
Village centre
☎ (53) 03 75 61
Do not miss the beautiful little village of Bourdeilles, near Brantôme. The Griffons has 10 rooms and good menus priced from F110 to F200. Recommended.

24310 Brantôme

L'AUBERGE DU SOIR
Town centre
☎ (53) 05 82 93
Brantôme is a Renaissance gem, set in the country north of Périgueux. This tiny *auberge* has only eight rooms but the food is first-class, with local dishes and menus priced from F73 to F190. Good wine list.

24260 La Bugue

HOTEL DU CHATEAU
Campagne
☎ (53) 06 23 50
A very fine hotel-restaurant with a beautiful dining room, at Campagne, just across the Vézère from La Bugue. Serves both sophisticated and regional food in a splendid setting. Menus from F115 to F250. Recommended.

AUBERGE DU PRE-SAINT
Village centre
☎ (53) 07 15 14
A small *logis*, so in summer you must book ahead. 10 rooms and local dishes are the main appeal. Menus from F60 to F225, and a very good wine list. Recommended.

40100 Dax

AU FIN GOURMET
3 Rue des Pénitents
☎ (58) 74 04 26
This little 1-star *logis* is well known for good food, as it should be with

a name like that. Regional dishes occur throughout the menus, which run from F56 to F175. 15 rooms. Recommended.

24250 Domme

HOTEL L'ESPLANADE
Town centre
☎ (53) 28 31 41
Domme is a beautiful *bastide*, set high above the Dordogne, and it is best to stay in the town because the trippers leave about six o'clock. This *logis* has 19 rooms and a very good restaurant with menus from F110 to F300. Recommended.

33330 St Emilion

HOSTELLERIE PLAISENCE
Place Clocher
☎ (57) 24 72 32
King John gave this town its first charter in the twelfth century and the British are still very welcome, especially in this excellent restaurant. Menus from F98 to F220. 12 rooms. Recommended.

64500 St Jean-de-Luz

HOTEL LA FAYETTE
Restaurant Kayola
18–20 Rue de la République
☎ (59) 26 17 74
A good, central *logis* with 17 rooms and a separate restaurant. Menus from F100 to F280. Good seafood and Basque dishes. Excellent wine list. Restaurant closed Sunday evening.

LEONIE
6 Rue Garat
☎ (59) 26 37 10
St-Jean-de-Luz – or just Luz, as most people seem to call it – is an old tuna port, full of good restaurants, but I have chosen Léonie's because I know it well, and it has a fine Basque cook, Ramuntxo Etchenic. Menus from F100 to F130, so not expensive.

64220 St-Jean-Pied-de-Port

HOTEL DES PYRENEES
19 Place du Général de Gaulle
☎ (59) 37 01 01
I have stayed at the Hôtel des Pyrénées often over the last 20 years

and never had a poor meal. Besides, the Arrambiles are so friendly. This very fine hotel has 25 rooms, good staff and a first-class restaurant, with menus from F130 to F320, plus an extensive *carte* and good wines. Recommended.

33500 Libourne

LE CHANZY
16 Rue Chanzy
☎ (57) 51 05 15
An Englishman, Roger de Libourne, founded this little port at the junction of the Dordogne and Garonne. The Chanzy is a small restaurant with menus from F60 to F125, and a good wine list. 4 rooms available if the local hotels are full.

40000 Mont de Marsan

HOTEL ZANCHETTIN
Rendez-vous des Boulistes
Ave de Villeneuve
☎ (58) 75 19 52
Mont de Marsan is a fine town of the Landes, close to the Pyrenees. This little 1-star *logis* has only nine rooms, but the restaurant is very popular with the locals, and you will dine well from menus ranging from F50 to F100.

24290 Montignac

HOTEL LE LASCAUX
109 Ave Jean Jaurès
☎ (53) 51 82 81
The real caves of Lascaux are closed, but the reproduction of Lascaux II is a very decent alternative, well worth seeing. This 1-star *logis* has 16 rooms and sound food on menus priced from F60 to F180. Recommended.

64120 St Palais

RESTAURANT DINDART
23 Rue Thiers
☎ (59) 65 72 42
St Palais is a grey little town on the Road to Compostela, with several good hotels such as Le Trinquet, and this excellent Basque restaurant, with waitresses in local costume. Good menus with prices from F45 to only F115. Highly recommended.

64310 St Pée-sur-Nivelle

HOTEL DE LA NIVELLE
Town centre
☎ (59) 54 50 15
St Pée is one of a clutch of attractive Basque villages set in the green mountains of the western Pyrenees. This large 30-room *logis* is noted for regional fare and has sound menus priced from F85 to F140. M. Berrotaran won the *Logis de France* Regional Cookery Award with his *foie de canard chaud aux pommes*. Try it.

47140 Penne d'Agenais

HOTEL DU COMMERCE
Restaurant le Moulin
Port de Penne
☎ (53) 41 21 34
Penne is a beautiful undiscovered place, topped by a spectacular castle. This small *logis*, the ideal centre for touring the area, has 14 rooms and good menus from F50 to F120.

24000 Périgueux

RESTAURANT DOMINO
21 Place Francheville
☎ (53) 08 25 80
The cuisine of Périgord in all its traditional excellence is available at this old posting inn in the centre of Périgueux. Duck, goose,*saumon à l'oseille*, all the expected dishes and an excellent cellar. Well-spaced menus from F69 to F198. Recommended.

24250 La Roque Gageac

LA BELLE ETOILE
On river promenade
☎ (53) 29 51 44
This little village, where many houses are carved out of the cliffs, lies beside the river and has several small hotels and restaurants. This one has 16 rooms and good menus priced from F90 to F220. Good wines. Recommended.

64310 Sare

HOTEL FAGOAGA-BARATCHARTEA
Quartier Ihalar
☎ (59) 54 20 48

In the Basque country, green and full of flowers, the only difficulty is the tongue-twisting names. This 20-room *logis* is set in a pretty village near Ascain and has good, well-prepared dishes on menus from F75 to F120. Highly recommended.

24200 Sarlat

HOTEL ST ALBERT
Place Pasteur
☎ (53) 59 01 09
This is the largest *logis* (61 rooms) in this marvellous medieval town, another essential sight of the Dordogne. Menus from F80 to F210.

HOTEL LA HOIRIE
La Giragne
☎ (53) 59 05 62
The Hôtel La Hoirie is a few minutes' drive from the centre of Sarlat, and offers a pool and very good food. I suggest the *ris de veau braises aux truffes*. 15 rooms and menus from F160 to F250. Not cheap but excellent value.

LA MADELEINE
1 Place de la Petite Rigaudie
☎ (53) 59 10 41
A fine restaurant in a fine old house, with a good cellar providing a wide range of wines and good Périgord dishes on menus priced from F100 to F250. Recommended for that special occasion.

24170 Siorac-en-Périgord

L'AUBERGE DE LA PETITE REINE
Near the bridge
☎ (53) 31 60 42
M. and Mme Duc own this long-established and popular *logis* set beside the Dordogne. 40 rooms and a pool, plus good Périgord food on menus from F80 to F160. Recommended. For a special night out, try dining at the Scholly, just up the road.

33780 Soulac-sur-Mer

L'HACIENDA
Ave du Perrier de Larsan
☎ (56) 09 81 34
A strange name to find in France, but then Soulac, north of Bordeaux on the Gironde peninsula, is a seaside resort, though one with historic roots. The English pilgrims to Compostela disembarked here to start

their journey across Aquitaine. Menus from F70 to F170. 12 rooms, really rather pleasant.

24340 Vieux-Mareuil

AUBERGE DE L'ETANG-BLEU
Village centre
☎ (53) 60 92 63
This little village, north of Périgueux, south of Nontron, has one small, 11-room *logis*, with a cuisine that pulls in the locals. Menus from F85 to F350. Excellent local dishes and wines from Bordeaux and Bergerac. Highly recommended.

MIDI-PYRENEES

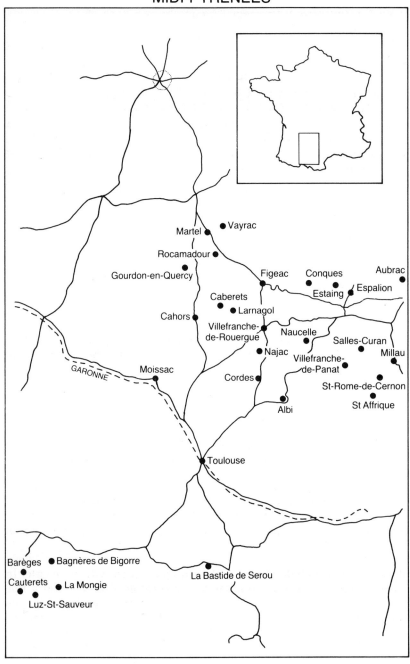

MIDI-PYRENEES

Midi-Pyrénées is a modern, composite region which overlaps, in part, the ancient Aquitaine but is now centred on the city of Toulouse. It contains seven diverse *départements*, which are, from the north-east to the south-west, Lot, Aveyron, Tarn, Tarn-et-Garonne, Haute-Garonne, Gers, Hautes-Pyrénées and Ariège. The historical link that would take any traveller right across this region is the Pilgrim Road from Le Puy to Compostela, which comes into the Midi-Pyrénées at the Lot and then runs north of Toulouse across the Gers and so south to the western Pyrenees. Modern travellers have a wider choice than this, and the access is easy, either via the airport at Toulouse-Blagnac, or by train, or the various autoroutes, notably the A62, which runs down the Garonne from Bordeaux.

Coming down from the north, the best way into the Midi-Pyrénées skirts to the east of the Dordogne and after a swift visit to the spectacular pilgrim town of Rocamadour, descends to the city of Cahors, capital of Quercy, which produces a very good wine and is well worth visiting for its famous bridge, the Pont Valentré. East of here lies the Lot Valley, and such places as the pilgrim town of Conques in the Aveyron, another little gem no true traveller should miss. In the Aveyron valley, a place off the too-well-trodden track, places to visit include Penne and Bruniquel, each with its castle. In Tarn-et-Garonne, pretty Moissac has several good hotels and a fine cathedral, and from there it is no great distance to Toulouse, the fourth largest city in France, a university town and a centre for the aircraft industry. Even so, my advice is to spend no more than a day here and then head west into the Armagnac country of the Gers. On the way west and south, visit Lectoure and Condom, and when in Condom drive out to the tiny little town, completely walled, of Larrissingle, before heading south for Tarbes and the Pyrenees. Places to see here, in the loom of the peaks, include Lourdes, the town of Ste-Bernadette, the spa town of Cauterets, and the great wall of the Cirque de Gavarnie, south of Luz-St-Sauveur, a real natural wonder. From here you can drive east, over the various cols, to Luchon and the abbey at St-Bertrand-de-Comminges. A good road, the D117, runs at the northern foot of the Pyrenees and takes you eventually into the Cathar country, the thirteenth-century home of the heretical Albigensian sect. Their last stronghold at Montségur in the Ariège is an imposing pile on a high mountain top, just one of many Cathar castles in the area.

Essential sights

The spa town of Cauterets in the Hautes-Pyrénées, with the Parc des Pyrénées higher up the road at Pont d'Espagne. Toulouse is worth a day, to see the cathedral of St Sernin. Auch is the old capital of the Gascons, and Larrissingle, near Condom, cannot be missed and is quite beautiful. Moissac has one of the finest examples of a cathedral tympanum in France, and Conques has the relics of Saint Foy and a cathedral treasure that dates back to Charlemagne. Lourdes is rather sad, full of sick people on pilgrimage, but south of here lies Luz and the riding and walking route up to the Cirque de Gavarnie. Around here lie the ski resorts of the Pyrenees, reached across the high cols, such as the Col de Tourmalet, on a spectacular mountain road.

Food

The food in Midi-Pyrénées is largely country fare, with a dash of the mountains, which means soups and stews rather than finely crafted dishes. There is trout and crayfish from the streams and lakes, and from Béarn the *poule au pot*. In Toulouse I recall that the *magret de canard*, duck sliced into small steaks, was particularly excellent, but much of the cooking in the north of the region is very similar to that of Aquitaine. Auch is a centre for *foie gras*. There are very good cheeses, such as the black Pyrenean cheese and the *Laruns* from Béarn, and a range of local dishes. *Alose de l'Adour* is shad, a small fish, stuffed with sorrel and ham; *daube à la Béarnaise* is beef in wine with onions and tomatoes.

Wine

The wines of the region come from several areas, but those of Cahors, the so-called 'black wine of Quercy' are particularly good. From just south of Armagnac, where the brandy comes from, there are the Madiran reds and further west the wines of Juraçon, which tend to be on the sweet side, and were said to have been offered to the newly born Henry of Navarre. Tarsan wines are hard to find but worth drinking when available. The great aperitif of the region is the *pousse-rapière*, the 'sword-thrust', a combination of Armagnac and sparkling white wine. Look out also for the wines of Gaillac, St Mont, and the Côtes du Frontonnais.

RESTAURANTS

12400 St Affrique

HOTEL MODERNE
54 Ave A. Pezet
☎ (65) 49 20 44
A beautiful little town of the southern Aveyron, St Affrique is well off the tourist track. Go there and stay in this charming 28-room *logis* and enjoy good food from menus priced from F52 to F210. Good wine list.

81000 Albi

LE VIEIL ALBY
25 Rue Toulouse-Lautrec
☎ (63) 54 14 69
A very small *logis*, with just eight rooms, in the town of Toulouse Lautrec, but the food is the thing. Excellent menus, with well-prepared local dishes and menus priced from F65 to F165. Albi has five *logis* of varying size, all very good.

12470 Aubrac

HOTEL MODERNE
Town centre
☎ (65) 44 28 42
One of the central points on the Road to Compostela from Le Puy, little Aubrac has several hotels and restaurants. This one, among the

largest, has 24 rooms and excellent food, with menus from F55 to F156. Recommended for all pilgrims.

65200 Bagnères de Bigorre

HOTEL FRASCATI
Boulevard Carnot
☎ (62) 95 21 14
Bagnères is a spa and a summer tourist centre, rather elegant for these parts. The name of this hotel seems a little odd but otherwise it is excellent, with 17 rooms and local dishes on menus priced from F50 to F130. Recommended.

HOTEL LES VIGNAUX
16 Rue de la République
☎ (62) 95 03 41
A smallish *logis* but the restaurant is notable, with excellent food on menus priced from F38 to a *gastronomique* F175. 14 rooms. Restaurant closed Monday outside high season.

63340 Barèges

HOTEL DE L'EUROPE
Town centre
☎ (62) 92 68 04
Barèges, close to La Mongie, via the Col du Tourmalet, is a ski resort and spa, with plenty of good restaurants, but you will dine well here at this 2-star, 51-room *logis*. Menus from F50 to F150. Recommended.

09290 La Bastide de Serou

HOTEL FERRE
Rue St Girons
☎ (61) 64 50 26
This 1-star *logis* is a regional winner of the *Logis de France* Cookery Competition with a marvellous local dish, *cassoulet au confit de canard*. Laura and Louis Debrieu, who run this little *logis*, have 10 rooms available and a well-chosen selection of dishes on menus priced from F50 to F110. Recommended.

46330 Caberets

AUBERGE DU SOMBRAL
Town centre
St Cirq Lapopie
☎ (65) 31 26 08

This 10-room *auberge* lies at the top of St Cirq Lapopie, a beautiful, straggling village of the Lot, and has a restaurant which the owner, M. Hardeveld, claims to be *plein de bonnes choses*, which it is, and you will find them on menus priced from F65 to F220. Not to be missed. Highly recommended.

46000 Cahors

HOTEL CHARTREUSE
Rue St Georges
☎ (65) 35 17 37
A 3-star *logis*, in the town centre, with 34 rooms, good menus priced from F55 to F160 and a wine list featuring the *bon Cahors* – the black wine of Quercy. If you don't like dark-red wines, I recommend the *Perlé* from Gaillac, which is particularly good in a *kir*. Restaurant closed Monday lunchtime.

HOTEL LE MELCHIOR
Place de la Gare
☎ (65) 35 03 38
This is an agreeable if far from beautiful hotel, with reliable food, menus from F53 to F155, and very helpful management. Restaurant closed Sunday. The hotel is recommended not least because it is very close to the famous Pont Valentré, the medieval bridge across the river.

LA TAVERNE
1 Rue J. B. Delpech
☎ (65) 35 28 66
I have been eating at the Taverne on and off since 1975 and have never had a bad meal there. Try the specialities such as the *saumon frais au Cahors*, or an *omelette aux cèpes*, or the *cassoulet* – and more of that fine local wine. Menus from F90 to F290. Excellent wine list. Recommended.

65110 Cauterets

LE PAS DE L'OURS
21 Rue de la Raillère
☎ (62) 92 58 07
Cauterets is a spa and ski resort, and seems to have no great interest in eating, so I chose this small 11-room *logis*, which serves regional, Pyrenean dishes on menus priced from F57 to F70. Good wine list. A resort town, Cauterets has 11 *logis*, so the choice is wide.

12320 Conques

HOTEL STE-FOY
Town centre
☎ (65) 69 84 03
The classic hotel of the Aveyron, and very well run. Not cheap but
good food and excellent wines. Expect to pay around F200 for dinner.
20 rooms.

AUBERGE ST JACQUES
Town centre
☎ (65) 72 86 36
Conques is a gem of a town. The cathedral holds the relics of Saint
Foy and the town was a major stop on the Road to Compostela. This
logis has 11 rooms and sound cooking, with menus priced from F55 to
F120.

AUBERGE DU PONT ROMAIN
Near the river bridge
☎ (65) 69 84 07
An American friend, Herb McGrew, who walked to Compostela, said
about this hotel, 'We enjoyed ourselves so much we stayed 2 nights.'
Huge, good, delightfully served meals, and if you can, stay in Room
37 or 47, just off the terrace. Seven rooms. Menus from F45 to F90.

81170 Cordes

LE GRAND ECUYER
Rue Voltaire
☎ (63) 56 06 03
Cordes, a medieval hilltop town, was falling into ruin when a group of
artisans moved in to live there and restore it. This hotel-restaurant is
in one of the medieval buildings. Pride of place must go to the
remarkably extensive wine list, but the menus, from F150 to F300,
though not cheap, are excellent. Highly recommended.

HOSTELLERIE DU PARC
Town centre
☎ (63) 56 02 59
This little 15-room hotel lies at the foot of the hill, outside the walls.
The fare is regional, very well prepared – for example *poularde farcie*
– delicious – or rabbit. Good wine list. Menus from F75 to F250.
Recommended.

12500 Espalion

HOTEL-RESTAURANT MODERN
27 Boulevard de Guizard
☎ (65) 44 05 11
M. Maulhac tells me they are going to do up this 2-star *logis*, but the
excellent dining room must not be changed a bit. This is a gastronomic find in the valley of the Lot, with excellent food on menus from
F85 to F200. 25 rooms. Highly recommended.

12190 Estaing

AUX ARMES D'ESTAING
Town centre
☎ (65) 44 70 02
Estaing is one of the most beautiful places in the Lot valley, topped by
a splendid castle. This *logis* tends to be crowded and the food may
suffer a little, but it is still excellent value. 44 rooms and menus from
F50 to F120.

46100 Figeac

HOTEL TERMINUS ST JACQUES
27 Ave Clemenceau
☎ (65) 34 00 43
This hotel is a stop on the Road to Compostela, as the name indicates,
and gives an especially warm welcome to Compostela-bound travellers. 12 rooms, so it is best to book. Good, reliable menus from F75 to
F150.

46300 Gourdon-en-Quercy

HOSTELLERIE DE LA BOURIANE
Place Foirail
☎ (65) 41 16 37
Friends of mine returned from the Lot, singing the praises of this
logis north of Cahors. 20 rooms and a fine restaurant, offering local
specialities. Menus from F75 to F200. Recommended.

46160 Larnagol

LE MAS DE CARITEAU
☎ (65) 31 28 77
This *logis* near Cajarc is set in an old country house – a *mas* – and has
30 rooms and good, well-prepared food on menus from F70 to F120.

65120 Luz-St-Sauveur

HOTEL BON ACCUEIL
Town centre
☎ (62) 92 80 39
No one can visit the Hautes-Pyrénées without seeing the soaring
cliffs of the Cirque de Gavarnie and the pass of the Brèche de Roland.
This hotel in pretty Luz, the nearest centre to the Cirque, has 18
rooms and inexpensive menus ranging from F60 to F100.

46600 Martel

RESTAURANT LE QUERCY
Hôtel Le Turenne
☎ (65) 37 30 30
Martel gets overshadowed by nearby Rocamadour, but is just as
striking in a quieter way, and well worth a visit. This excellent 2-star
logis with 17 rooms, near the house where the son of Henry II of
England died, offers first-class food on menus priced from F90 to
F220.

12000 Millau

HOTEL DES CAUSSES
56 Ave Jean Jaurès
☎ (65) 60 03 19
My daughter and I stayed in this *logis* during our cycle ride across
France and were made very welcome by M. and Mme Fernandez. We
soared up the side of the Causse de Larzac next day with no trouble.
22 rooms and menus from F50 to F120. Recommended.

82200 Moissac

LE PONT NAPOLEON
2 Allée Montebello
☎ (63) 04 01 55
Local food is the basis of the dishes here. Good wines, menus from F95
to F225, and 13 rooms. Recommended.

65200 La Mongie

LE PIC D'ESPADE HOTEL
Village centre
☎ (62) 91 92 27

A highly regarded 2-star *logis* in the mountains of the Hautes-Pyrénées. 28 rooms and reasonable menus priced from F65 to F75. La Mongie is a ski resort, rather modern and not very attractive, but the mountains round about are quite spectacular.

12270 Najac

L'OUSTAL DEL BARRY
Place du Bourg
☎ (65) 29 74 32
Najac is a splendid little town with a classic ruined castle. This excellent *logis* is the place to stay, with its 21 rooms and first-class food on menus from F95 to F250. Recommended.

12800 Naucelle

HOTEL UNAL
Town centre
☎ (65) 69 21 21
It is some years since I visited this village in the Aveyron, but I remember this hotel for its warm welcome and a very fine dinner. There are 12 rooms and menus priced from F45 to F150. Restaurant closed Sunday evening and Monday.

46500 Rocamadour

HOTEL TERMINUS
Place de la Carreta
☎ (65) 33 62 14
A small, unpretentious *logis* in the town, with 15 rooms and menus priced from F52 to F100.

LES VIEILLES TOURS
On D673
☎ (65) 33 68 01
Rocamadour is a famous shrine and one of the sights of the Lot, but a terrible tourist trap. Look and leave is my advice, certainly in July and August, but this tiny *logis*, a mile from the town on the D673, has seven rooms and very good food. Menus from F70 to F120.

12490 St-Rome-de-Cernon

HOTEL DU COMMERCE
Town centre
☎ (65) 62 33 92
A little town below the Causse de Larzac, hard to find, where this friendly *logis* made me very welcome when I was quite worn out on a very hot day in August; a beautiful spot. 13 rooms and good, plain cooking. Menus from F50 to F100.

12410 Salles-Curan

HOSTELLERIE DU LEVEZOU
Town centre
☎ (65) 46 34 16
Salles is very close to a huge lake – an inland sea. This *logis* has only 14 rooms but first-class food and wine. Menus from F80 to F300. Recommended. This area, south of Rodez, sees very few British visitors and deserves more attention.

31000 Toulouse

LE BISTRO VAN GOGH
21 Place St Georges
☎ (61) 21 03 15
A very lively, long-established brasserie-style restaurant, with an open terrace onto the *place*. Good seafood, duck and steaks. Menus from F60 to F110.

LE COLOMBIER
14 Rue Bayard
☎ (61) 62 40 05
A good range of wines and the *cassoulet* are the chief attractions of this friendly restaurant, long popular with the locals. Menus from F70 to F175. Recommended.

RESTAURANT DANOZE
19 Rue Castellane
☎ (61) 62 34 70
This is one of the great restaurants of Toulouse. But, like all great restaurants, it is not cheap – eating from the *carte* can well exceed F500 a head. However, if you stay with the menus, which range from F125 to F280, you will do very well.

46110 Vayrac

HOSTELLERIE FENELON
Carennac
☎ (65) 38 67 67
Four of my friends found this excellent restaurant and I see from their bill that lunch, with two on the F55 menu and two on the F80 menu, plus a bottle of Buzet cost F318 – say £30. Excellent value, and, according to them, very good food. Carennac is a pretty place. Eat here when you visit it.

12430 Villefranche-de-Panat

HOSTELLERIE DU LAC
Village centre
☎ (65) 46 58 07
A fine *logis* near the great lake south of Rodez. 20 rooms and good menus from F55 to F150.

12200 Villefranche-de-Rouergue

RELAIS DE FARROU
2½ miles along road to Figeac
☎ (65) 45 18 11
This is a small roadside *logis*, with just 14 rooms, and really excellent food. The host, M. Boulliard, is very kind to cyclists. Menus from F70 to F210 and excellent wines. Restaurant closed Sunday evening and Tuesday.

LANGUEDOC-ROUSSILLON

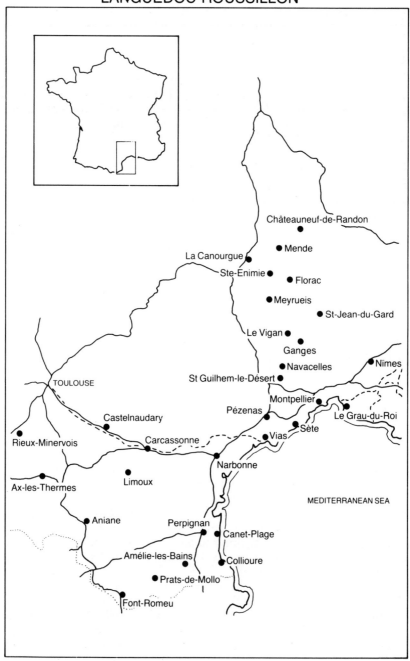

Châteauneuf-de-Randon

● Mende

La Canourgue
Ste-Enimie
● Florac

● Meyrueis

St-Jean-du-Gard

Le Vigan
Ganges
● Navacelles

Nîmes

TOULOUSE

St Guilhem-le-Désert

Montpellier

Pézenas

Le Grau-du-Roi

Castelnaudary

Sète

Rieux-Minervois

Carcassonne

Vias

Narbonne

Ax-les-Thermes

Limoux

MEDITERRANEAN SEA

Aniane

Perpignan

Canet-Plage

Amélie-les-Bains

Collioure

Prats-de-Mollo

Font-Romeu

LANGUEDOC-ROUSSILLON

Not so many years ago, Languedoc-Roussillon was virtually un-known to the summer holidaymaker, not least because the lakes and marshes that lie behind the coast of the Golfe du Lion were home to a particularly ferocious breed of mosquito, and the hills of the hinter-land were crossed only by narrow roads and rough tracks. Then, in the mid-1960s, all that began to change. A concentrated spraying campaign eradicated the mosquito and the developers moved in to build a string of resorts down the coast: La Grande Motte, Agde, Port-Leucate, Barcarès, Canet and several more around and along the great sandy beaches of the Golfe du Lion, and the hills of the Cévennes and the Espinouse began to attract walkers and campers.

Personally, I don't care much for modern resorts, but fortunately Languedoc-Roussillon also has a great deal to offer the historically-minded traveller. It has two cultures, a great deal of magnificent scenery, and a number of beautiful towns. Lovers of the coast or the country will both find something to enjoy in this exquisite, unsophis-ticated corner of France, while as a bonus, the weather is benign and the wine ever-more palatable.

The modern Languedoc-Roussillon is made up of five *départements*: Pyrénées-Orientales, on the Spanish frontier, the home of the French Catalans; then comes most of the old County of Toulouse, now the *départements* of Aude, Hérault, Gard and, in the north-east, moun-tainous Lozère, which contains the wild Cévennes. There is easy access to the region by road or rail, with two autoroutes, the A61 and the A9, via the Rhône valley or Toulouse, and airports, at Perpignan, Toulouse, Montpellier and Nîmes. The most famous route hereabouts must be the Canal du Midi, that classic waterway which links Toulouse to the Mediterranean by the port of Sète.

Coming in from the west, down the road from Toulouse, I advise a stop at the main port of Castelnaudary on the Canal du Midi, and then half a day at least for the fortress city of Carcassonne, which has been restored to its full medieval glory and must not be missed. Turn off here, south for Limoux, where they produce a fine sparkling wine, the *Blanquette de Limoux*, and so into Roussillon, across the foothills of the Pyrenees. Visit pretty Prades, once the home of the cellist Pablo Casals, and then climb up the steep, winding road, high above the vine-draped coastal plains to the airy green plateau of the Cerdagne, 6000 ft above the sea, for it is an alpine paradise of flowers and meadows. Not many people go up there and it really is quite beautiful.

Back down on the plain, head along the D115 for Céret, where the cherry blossom blows about like snow in the springtime. Back on the Mediterranean coast you can skip all the other places, but do not miss pretty Collioure, which has a Roman *phare*, or lighthouse, and lots of quayside restaurants and, except in July and August, when it is packed, is quite divine. Elne has a very fine church, but spare two days or so for Perpignan, where you must go to the Place de la Loge in the evening and watch people rise from the cafe tables to dance the *Sardane*, the great folk-dance of Catalonia. Inland from here, past Thuirs, lies the little hill town of Castelnou, well off the beaten track but not to be missed. On the road north, a visit to the great castle at Salses is another worthwhile diversion, before the hills of the Corbières loom up to the west.

Heading north up the coast, Narbonne is a fine old town, but Béziers is even finer, and hosts a great wine festival in August. Moving on, there is Pézenas, so beautiful and so authentically sixteenth century that it is often used as a film set; it was once the home of Molière. Old Agde, on the coast, is much nicer than Cap d'Agde, half of which is a nudist resort, but for choice go directly to Sète, built by Colbert as the southern port of the Canal du Midi and now the busiest wine port in France. To complete the coastal route, go to Vias on the Canal du Midi and then press on to the university city of Montpellier, one of the finest of all the French provincial towns, and then on to the Crusader port of Aigues-Mortes, built by St Louis in the thirteenth century and still completely walled, set on the salt-pans by the works of the Salins du Midi.

Once here, on the edge of the Camargue, either head north of

Montpellier towards the distant Cévennes, first to St Guilhem-le-Désert, a gem of a village, then up the Hérault river through Ganges and Le Vigan, or turn east into the Camargue. In the Cévennes, descend into the vast hole of the Cirque de Navacelles – there is a good restaurant on the bottom – and then go up onto the Causse de Larzac to the little Knights Templar town of La Couvoirrade. Finally, in this north-eastern part of Lozère, visit Anduse, Alès and St-Jean-du-Gard, and take a drive along the Corniche des Cévennes to pretty Florac, Mende and Marvejols, perfect walking or car-touring country.

Across the Causse de Larzac to the west lies Millau, and not far from there the maturing caves for Roquefort cheese. Press on towards Albi, a famous town, once the home of Toulouse-Lautrec, and try the wines of Gaillac, before heading up to the medieval town of Cordes and so out of the region. Languedoc-Roussillon is a fabulous region and, especially if you explore the wilder parts behind the coast, you will discover a countryside still uncluttered by tourists, very beautiful and quite unspoiled.

Essential sights

Walled Carcassonne must be seen, as must Aigues-Mortes in the Camargue. Béziers and Montpellier are very fine towns, Montpellier being the more attractive. Perpignan is very lively. A cruise on the Canal du Midi is a very good idea, or you can continue to follow Robert Louis Stevenson's route on his *Travels with a Donkey in the Cévennes* from Florac to St-Jean-du-Gard. I recommend a visit to Sète for the quayside restaurants and the beaches. Collioure in Roussillon is beautiful, and for something strange visit the village of Rennes-le-Château near Quillan, and for somewhere beautiful, walled Castelnau, near Thier. Albi is worth a stop, as is Cordes, and the Cirque de Navacelles is simply breathtaking. The list is endless, but at least mark these places on your map and see as many as you can.

Food

My favourite dish in the Languedoc is a simple *tielle*, a fish pasty, bought hot from one of the stalls on the quay at Sète and consumed with a glass or two of chilled Listel rosé – delicious. In Castelnaudary, *caussoulet*, a casserole of beans and goose and bacon, is the great dish, and there is good fish and shellfish all along the coast, including excellent mussels, *moules*, from the Etang de Thau, behind Sète. Ham from the mountains and lamb from the *causses* are found on many menus, but the most famous produce hereabouts is surely Roquefort cheese, the king of all soft *bleu* cheeses, sharp and delicious, although the *Bleu de Causse* of Florac is very good, as is the *pelardon* goat's cheese of the Cévennes. Among fish dishes, the *brandade de morue*, salt cod in a cream and garlic sauce, is the local speciality, and while on the subject of garlic, be aware that *aïoli*, garlic mayonnaise, pops up everywhere.

Wine

The wines of Languedoc-Roussillon used to be little more than 'plonk', but they have improved a great deal in recent years as new varieties of grape are introduced. The region now produces a great deal of very palatable wine, and to give a few favourites, I usually drink the reds from the Côtes du Roussillon, the Listel *gris-de-gris* rosé from the Camargue, and the white Gaillac *perlé* from the country near Albi. If you do the same, you will not go far wrong. There are fortified wines from Banyuls, and Muscat from around Frontignan, and the aperitif Rivesaltes from near Salses. Some say that the red wine of Collioure is the best *vin de table* in the region. In the Aude there are three distinct wine regions: Minervois, Corbières and the less-well-known Fitou, mostly reds, with the sparkling *Blanquette de Limoux* as the great party wine of the region. There are two AC wines in the Hérault, of which the St Chinian is my favourite, and lots of wine under the Côtes du Languedoc label. The white wine from La Clape is very good, and for a good unpretentious *vin de pays* from a vast local choice, try the inexpensive *vin de pays de l'Herault*. The Languedoc is now the largest wine-producing area in France, and while the wines cannot be regarded as classics, they are quite good and getting better.

RESTAURANTS

66110 Amélie-les-Bains

HOTEL CENTRAL
Town centre
☎ (68) 39 05 49
M. Sitja, who runs this excellent hotel in the spa town of Amélie in the eastern Pyrenees – Roussillon – has won a host of awards for his cooking, including the 1987 *Logis de France* Local Cookery award. Menus from F65 to F100, so not expensive. 28 rooms. Even without the hotel and M. Sitja's cooking, Amélie is well worth a diversion.

34150 Aniane

HOSTELLERIE ST BENOIT
Route de St Guilhem
☎ (67) 57 71 63
A newly built, very attractive *logis*, close to Sète, where Mme Raoul
speaks good English and runs a fine half-terraced restaurant by the
pool. Menus from F85 to F200. 30 rooms.

09110 Ax-les-Thermes

HOTEL LE CHALET
☎ (61) 64 24 31
A good 2-star *logis* in this little spa town. Good food and well-assorted
menus from F60 to F120. 10 rooms. As the full name implies, Ax is a
spa town, with bracing air and lots of good walks in the hills round
about.

66140 Canet-Plage

LE DON QUICHOTTE
22 Ave de Catalogne
☎ (68) 80 35 17
A good small restaurant, serving a range of attractive dishes, including many Catalan dishes and excellent seafood, on menus ranging
from F65 to F140. ·

48500 La Canourgue

HOTEL DU COMMERCE
Town centre
☎ (66) 32 80 18
M. Mirmand is a superb chef who won the *Logis de France* regional
heat for Languedoc-Roussillon with his *La Pouteille*, which I can best
describe as a stew – the recipe is given in verse. There are 30 rooms
and good menus from F50 to F100. The mountains of Lozère are very
attractive, and this hotel would make an excellent touring base.

11000 Carcassonne

LOGIS DE TRENCAVEL
290 Ave Général Leclerc
☎ (68) 71 09 53
I approve of hotels with a limited number of rooms, as the food tends
to be good. This is certainly the case here, where there are only 12
rooms – the menus, offering excellent food and good value, range from
F120 to F225.

HOTEL DU DONJON
2 Rue Comte Roger
☎ (68) 71 08 80
Carcassonne is full of hotels and has several *logis*, but this one is not only set inside the old *cité*, within the medieval walls, it also serves excellent food on a F100 menu. 36 rooms. Restaurant closed Sunday.

11400 Castelnaudary

HOTEL DU CENTRE
31 Cours de la République
☎ (68) 23 25 95
Cassoulet is the great dish of Castelnaudary – they even advertise it with *ses églises* as one of the town's attractions. This hotel has 17 rooms and *cassoulet* is among the dishes included on their menus, which run from F60 to F220.

66300 Castelnou

L'OUSTAL (OR L'HOSTAL)
Village centre
☎ (68) 53 45 42
Castelnou is a marvellous fortified village in the country near Thuirs, and is not to be missed when touring Roussillon. L'Oustal is a small restaurant with terrace tables, set in the centre, serving such dishes as a *cargolade* of grilled snails. Good local wines served in jugs. Menus from F80 to F160, wine included.

48170 Châteauneuf-de-Randon

HOTEL LA POSTE
L'Habitarelle
☎ (66) 47 90 05
The great patriot-soldier of France, Bertrand du Guesclin, died besieging the walls of Châteauneuf, and his effigy still lies before the gates. This fine hotel of Lozère has 23 rooms and menus priced from F40 to F110.

66190 Collioure

LA BODEGA
Rue République
☎ (68) 82 05 60
Collioure is a beautiful little seaport and resort, full of restaurants. This is my personal favourite. Menus priced from F75 to F185,

excellent seafood and a good wine list. Do not miss Collioure or this restaurant.

48201 Ste-Enimie

HOTEL DE PARIS
On the river promenade
☎ (66) 48 50 02
A fine hotel by the banks of the Tarn, in this lovely little pilgrim town. 15 rooms and good food on menus from F75 to F125. The famous Gorges du Tarn lie on either side of the town, and the *causse* country of Languedoc lies to the north and south. Although crowded in July and August, this town is an ideal touring centre at all other times.

48400 Florac

HOTEL LE ROCHEFORT
On Route Nationale 106
☎ (66) 45 02 57
Florac is a pretty town, convenient for the Cévennes, set on the Robert Louis Stevenson Trail. This 24-room *logis* has a notably good restaurant, with menus from F65 to F150. Try the local cheese, the *bleu de causse*, or the fresh-caught trout from the river.

66120 Font-Romeu

HOTEL-RESTAURANT LE COQ HARDI
Rue de la République
Odeillo
☎ (68) 30 11 02
A very good *logis* at Odeillo, half a mile from the ski centre at Font-Romeu on the 6000-ft Cerdagne plateau above Perpignan. 23 rooms, good menus from F65 to F150. The Cerdagne plateau is a marvellous place, a little Switzerland high above the dusty Languedoc plain, and well worth a visit, perhaps on *Le Petit Train Jaune*, the 'Little Yellow Train' that runs up from the Conflent Valley below.

34190 Ganges

AUX CAVES DE L'HERAULT
14 Rue Jeu de Ballon
☎ (67) 73 81 09
A very comfortable town-centre *logis* with 13 rooms and a pleasant terraced restaurant which offers good food and chilled Listel wine. Menus from F55 to F110. Restaurant closed Friday evening and Saturday outside high season.

30240 Le Grau-du-Roi

LE SPINAKER
Route du Môle
Port Camargue
☎ (66) 51 54 93
The Spinaker is a very fine restaurant, well known in the area and well worth a visit while holidaying hereabouts in the Gard. Good fish, fine cellar. Menus from F169 to F270.

34150 St Guilhem-le-Désert

HOTEL FONZES
Town centre
☎ (67) 57 72 01
A beautiful quiet little town tucked into the wild hills of the Hérault near Gignac. This *logis* has 10 rooms and excellent food on menus ranging from F80 to F170. Stay on a while here, if possible, to enjoy walking in the hills or bathing in the nearby River Hérault – the perfect way to spend a hot summer day.

30270 St-Jean-du-Gard

AUBERGE DU PERAS
Route de Nîmes
☎ (66) 85 35 94
St-Jean-du-Gard is the central village of the Cévennes, a pretty spot with several good hotels. This one serves local dishes, including wild boar, on menus from F55 to F165. Only 10 rooms. Robert Louis Stevenson finished his *Travels with a Donkey* in St-Jean, and many walkers do so today, after walking from the distant Vélay.

11300 Limoux

LA MAISON DE LA BLANQUETTE
Promenade du Tivoli
☎ (68) 31 01 63
Sparkling *Blanquette de Limoux* is the great party wine of the Languedoc. This pleasant little restaurant on the Aude serves this wine and very good food on menus from F60.

HOTEL MODERNE-ET-PIGEON
1 Plage Général Leclerc
☎ (68) 31 00 25
One of three *logis* in this little town near Carcassonne, with 23 rooms and excellent local food. Menus priced from F75 to F175. Limoux is a good place to visit or stay in when Carcassonne is crowded.

48000 Mende

HOTEL DU PONT-ROUPT
Ave 11 Novembre
☎ (66) 65 01 43
Mende is a small town north of the Cévennes, a centre for northern Lozère, with several good *logis*. This one is a large, friendly establishment by the bridge – a stop on my walk through France – with 37 rooms and good menus priced from F70 to F170. The local dishes include *tripoux*, a kind of haggis. Good wine list.

48150 Meyrueis

HOTEL FAMILY
Town centre
☎ (66) 45 60 02
When I stopped in this hotel on my walk across France they were taking the roof off to add another storey. Now the hotel offers 48 rooms, as well as a warm welcome from the Julian family. A good time certainly awaits you at this 2-star *logis* in the Jonte valley of the Cévennes. Menus from F65 to F145. Highly recommended.

34000 Montpellier

L'OLIVIER
12 Rue Aristide Olivier
☎ (67) 92 86 28
Montpellier is one of the finest provincial cities in France, with a beautiful central square and an ancient university. This restaurant has Michel Breton's ever-improving cooking and excellent menus from F95 to F150, and *carte*. Closed during August, and Sunday and Monday at other times.

11000 Narbonne

HOTEL CROQUE-CAILLE
Route de Perpignan
☎ (68) 41 29 69
This 2-star *logis*, with local specialities in the restaurant, lies 2 miles south of the town. Only 10 rooms, so it is essential to book in summer. Menus from F50 to F120. Restaurant closed Sunday.

l34520 Navacelles (Cirque de)

AUBERGE DE LA CASCADE
Centre Cirque
☎ (67) 81 50 95

The Cirque de Navacelles is a great hole in the earth, a natural wonder, which must be seen by anyone touring in this part of France. The *auberge* lies by the river at the bottom and has only five rooms, so it is essential to book. Good menus from F75 to F125.

30000 Nîmes

L'ALBERGUIER
4 Rue Racine
☎ (66) 36 13 22
A very good local restaurant in this fine old Roman town, which still has a complete amphitheatre, full of Roman remains. The fish and seafood are particularly fine. Menus from F90 to F160. Good wine list.

66000 Perpignan

L'APERO
40 Rue de la Fusterie
☎ (68) 51 21 14
People dance the *sardane*, the great folk-dance of Catalonia, every evening near the Place de la Loge in Perpignan – well worth seeing. Dine first at this attactive, traditional restaurant. Try the *rognons de veau*, and some of the desserts. Good wine list. *Carte* only – expect to pay from F200.

34120 Pézenas

LE PRE SAINT-JEAN
18 Ave du Maréchal Leclerc
☎ (67) 98 15 81
An agreeable little restaurant in this classic seventeenth–eighteenth century town, which all visitors to Languedoc should visit – it was once the home of Molière. This restaurant has good, varied menus – fish, veal, poultry – priced from F85 to F200. Good wine list.

66230 Prats-de-Mollo

LA CREMAILLIERE
Route de Preste
☎ (68) 39 70 62
Prats is another fine little town at the foot of the Roussillon Pyrenees. Menus from F60 to F100, so not expensive. Rooms available.

HOSTELLERIE DE RELAIS
3 Place de la Trinxeria
☎ (68) 39 71 30
A small *logis* in this attractive town, close to the eastern end of the

◀————————————————————————————▶

Pyrenees, with 15 rooms and good menus from F50 to F110. Restaurant closed January.

11160 Rieux-Minervois

LOGIS DE MERINVILLE
Town centre
☎ (68) 78 11 78
Rieux is in the centre of the Minervois wine district, east of Carcassonne. This tiny *logis*, with just eight rooms, relies on its restaurant, which serves excellent food in great variety on menus priced from F50 to F120. Good Minervois wines, naturally. Restaurant closed Tuesday and Wednesday evening.

34200 Sète

LE RIVE GAUCHE
14 Quai Noel Guignon
☎ (67) 74 40 59
Sète is full of good seafood restaurants along its quays, so any choice is difficult, but this one stands among the best. Duck is also a speciality, and the menus are priced from F65 to F170. Good wine list. If you only want a snack in Sète, try a hot *tielle*, a fish pie, which you can purchase at any one of the stalls at the seaward end of the quay.

34450 Vias

HOTEL MYRIAM
Vias Plage
☎ (67) 21 64 59
Vias is a village on the Canal du Midi, in the Hérault, with several good small restaurants and this excellent *logis*, with 24 rooms and reasonably priced menus from F65 to F100.

30120 Le Vigan

HOTEL DES VOYAGEURS
12 Place du Quai
☎ (67) 81 00 34
Le Vigan is a small town at the southern edge of the Cévennes. This hotel has 14 rooms and menus from F60 to F100. I stayed here at the end of my walk across France, having made a very difficult crossing of the Cévennes, and M. Gomez and his staff made me very welcome. A pleasant *logis*, highly recommended.

◀————————————————————————————▶

PROVENCE – COTE D'AZUR – CORSICA

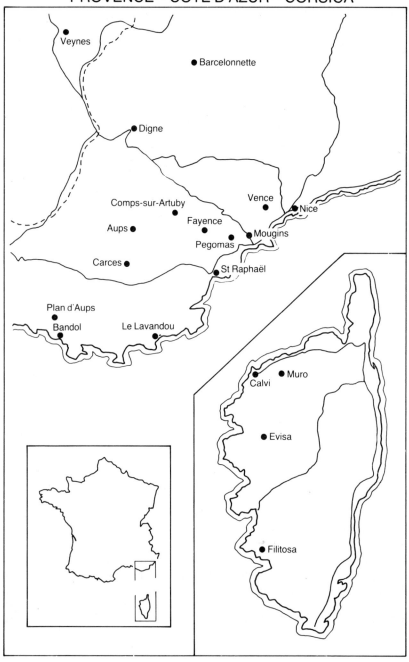

PROVENCE, COTE D'AZUR AND CORSICA

These three – the province, regions and county of Provence, the Côte d'Azur and the island of Corsica – have this much in common: they are all part of the same geological strata and have similar terrain. All three are sea-girt and mountainous, with a rocky soil cloaked with gorse, lavender, dwarf oaks, *garrigue* and *maquis*. All three areas enjoy good weather, with long hot summers and mild winters, but culturally they are diverse. The Corsicans are scarcely French at all, the Niçois were Italian until the last century, and the Provençals and Méridionals of southern France are rather different from the French you find north of, say, Valence, where the Midi is said to begin.

This part of France is a holiday region *par excellence*, but most of the heavy holiday traffic stays along the Riviera on the fabled and fabulous Côte d'Azur, and so I want to suggest that true travellers should also head inland to parts of the *arrière-pays*, behind the coast and not simply restrict their travels to those pretty places between Marseille and Monte Carlo.

These three areas are now made up of eight *départements*: in Provence, Bouches-du-Rhône, Var, Vaucluse, Hautes-Alpes and Alpes-de-Haute-Provence; Alpes-Maritimes, which covers the entire Côte d'Azur; and in Corsica, Haute-Corse and Corse-du-Sud. Access to all parts is easy, with airports at Nice, Marseille, Toulon, Bastia and Ajaccio, fast TGV trains from Paris, a good autoroute network, notably the A8, and regular ferries to Corsica from the ports of Nice, Marseille and Toulon.

As alays in rural France, it pays to tour by car, although the coastal parts of the Riviera can be explored quite easily using the coastal railway line. To suggest just a few of the many sights, the following route would be enjoyable. Coming in from the north, stop first at Avignon, the city of the Popes, and from there visit Tarascon on the banks of the Rhône, and parts of the Camargue. Other places around Avignon which will repay a close look include the Roman city of Orange, the heights of Mont Ventoux and the mysterious rock formations at Les Baux. Marseille is a big, bustling, thriving city and sea-port, but for something smaller visit the abbey at St Maximin or the city of Gauguin and Van Gogh, Aix-en-Provence, which has a university and is therefore rather lively. Apt is the capital of the *département* of the Vaucluse, and another fine town, but the country-side is the real attraction, a place of small villages where the narrow streets are lined with shady plane trees, and the hills shimmer in the summer sun, cloaked with flowers and purple lavender. The *villages-perchés* of the Var, such as Fayence, are also worth visiting.

Down on the coast and moving east, try Cassis and Bandol, more truly French than St Tropez or modern Port Grimaud, and then cross the Massif de St Baume to Toulon into the Massif de Maures, which rises behind the resort of Le Lavandou. Skirting St Tropez brings the traveller to the classic Riviera, St Raphaël, Cannes, La Napoule, Juan-les-Pins, Golfe Juan. Before Nice, turn into the hills to see Cagnes, the delightful town of St-Paul-de-Vence, Eze and Cap-Ferrat, before dropping in at Monte Carlo and then arriving at Menton on the Italian frontier.

This coast road along the Corniche done, go inland, into the Alpes-Maritimes. You can do this by a little train, the *Chemin de Fer de Provence*, which runs into the hills from the centre of Nice and all the way round to Digne, through hill villages such as Annot and Entre-vaux. Further inland, Castellane is a fine little town, close to the great gorge or 'canyon' of Verdon, but once here in the hills, just wander about and find your own special places. You won't regret it, for the views alone are worth the journey.

A car is also essential on Corsica, but be aware that on the narrow, winding roads a place you can see just across the valley can take three hours to reach by road. The train ride to Corte, in the north, is a famous excursion, and I for one prefer the northern part of the island. I recommend in particular the drive up the Cap-Corse, north of Bastia. Around the coast, Calvi, Porto and Propriano are well worth a trip, and if you start in the north, you could finish in the south at the port of Bonifacio, returning up the east coast through Porto Vecchio, the hill town of Zonza and over the spine of the island back to Ajaccio. The birthplace of Napoleon, Corsica is a very wild and beautiful island, very 'French' for all the locals' efforts to prevent assimilation, and especially worth visiting in the spring.

Essential sights

There is something for everyone in these three areas, but to catch the best of each, in Provence I recommend a visit to the Camargue, Arles, a fine Roman city, and the rock formations of Les Baux. Aix-en-Provence and Apt are agreeable, artistic towns, and for a good coastal resort I suggest Sanary. Marseille is worth a visit, as is the quay at St Tropez, if only for an evening. In the Var and Alpes-Maritimes, St-Paul-de-Vence and Eze are outstanding. Take a trip on the *Chemin de Fer de Provence* from Nice to Digne, and if you like the mountains, visit the Parc de Mercantour. If you like glitz, try Cannes or Monte Carlo.

In Corsica, the train ride to Corte is a must. The very fit can walk the GR20 across the island. On the coast visit Porto Vecchio, the Cap-Corse and Propriano. Inland go to Sartène and Zonza.

Food

The Côte d'Azur ranks third after Paris and Lyon for good food and good restaurants. Some might say second after Paris, and if so, why argue? In the haunts of the Riviera glitterati you may pay dearly for your meals, but if you move inland and follow my advice, you can live like a king at no great cost.

Herbs, such as thyme, rosemary, sage and basil, with tomatoes and onions, are the basis of Provençal cooking, but its secret is the olive oil, from those olive trees that cloak so many of the hillsides. To begin with the most famous dish, try the fish stew, *bouillabaisse*, a speciality of Marseille, though found everywhere, even inland. Nice has the *salade Niçoise*, made with beans, anchovies, tomatoes, eggs and black olives. Fish dishes appear everywhere and range from red mullet to sardines to anchovies. Stews are also common, with the *daube* being usually excellent. Garlic seems to get into everything, including *aïoli*, the local mayonnaise. Among typical dishes one must also list ratatouille, and Italian dishes with French overtones, such as *pissaladière*, a kind of pizza. Typical dishes to look out or include *boeuf en daube*, a stew with red wine, sea urchins (*oursins*) in a soup called *oursinade*, *soupe au pistou*, a flavoursome fish soup, *loup au fenouil,* sea-bass in a fennel sauce. Spaghetti and ravioli dishes are also common on many menus, reflecting the proximity of Italy.

Corsica, like many mountain regions, relies on simple fare, but local dishes worth trying include *cabri* – roast kid, *prissuta*, mountain ham, lots of game-birds – some, alas, song birds, and a lot of veal. The best choice is probably seafood, which is always fresh and can be excellent. In addition to this variety of cuisine, there is an abundance of fresh fruit and vegetables, and a very high standard of cooking. Cheeses include *Tomme Banon,* Brousse de la Vesubie, and the sheep's milk *Tomme de Camargue,* or, in Corsica, the *Broccio.* You will see a great variety of cheese in all the markets.

Wine

There is a great deal of drinkable, if often unremarkable wine, produced all over the Midi. By far the best comes from the southern Côtes-du-Rhône, of which Châteauneuf-du-Pape is the best known, closely followed by Giocondas, both of which are excellent, full-bodied reds. In Provence there is the wine from the Côtes-de-Provence, the Côtes-de-Luberon, and several other Côtes. The best of these are rosé, and most of it is VDQS. My own favourite is the dry Listel *gris-de-gris* rosé, which actually comes from the Languedoc but appears on every list in Provence and goes with everything. Other good rosés come from Taval and Lirac. Along the coast in the Var and Vauclus there are good drinkable wines from Bandol, my own favourite, and adequate wines from the Côtes de Provence. Wines from the Luberon are the Côteaux de Pierrevert, which are also quite acceptable. For a dessert wine, or as an aperitif, try Baumes-de-Venise.

The Corsican vineyards are said to be the oldest in France – at least by the Corsicans. Most of it is the *Vin de Pays de l'Ile de Beauté,* but look out in particular for the wines from Calvi, Côteaux d'Ajaccio, Patrimonio and Sartène.

RESTAURANTS

83630 Aups

HOTEL LES CAVALETS
Bauduen
☎ (94) 70 08 64
This 2-star *logis* lies outside the village of Bauduen, close to the Ste-

Croix lake and the entrance to the Verdon Gorges. There is a swimming pool and a footpath to the lake, which has the dining room over it. Local dishes are a feature of the F95 to F200 menus. 20 rooms.

83150 Bandol

LA KER MOCOTTE
Rue Raimu
☎ (94) 29 46 53
This is one of four *logis* in Bandol, and I have chosen to feature it here because it has a pleasant restaurant and a good spread of menus priced from F110 to F180. It serves all the local specialities, many of them based on fish fresh-caught at the harbour.

AUBERGE DU PORT
9 Allée Jean Moulin
☎ (94) 29 42 63
This excellent restaurant opposite the busy port at Bandol offers the superb cooking of Serge Fricaud, once of the famous Moulin de Mougins. The seafood is marvellous – try the *coquilles St-Jacques*, or the *soupe de poissons*. Menus from F150 to F235.

04400 Barcelonnette

HOTEL DE L'AUPILLON
Route de St Pons
☎ (92) 81 01 09
A very small 1-star *logis* of Haute-Provence, with just seven rooms and menus from F70 to F110. It serves very good food at no great cost and demonstrates that where the restaurant is important to the income because of the small number of hotel rooms, the results can be outstanding.

LA FERME DE LA RENTE
Route de Super-Sauze
☎ (92) 81 08 39
A pleasant restaurant in an old farmhouse, with good menus from F70 to F150. Good dishes including *faux-filet à la moelle*, and excellent hams and pâtés.

83570 Carces

HOTEL LOU CALEN
Town centre
Cotignac
☎ (94) 04 60 40
Set in a hill village of the Var, north of Brignoles and the A8

autoroute, this 10-room hotel serves excellent local dishes, such as *soupe pistou* and *jambon d'Aups*. Menus from F100 to F220. Restaurant closed Wednesday.

83840 Comps-sur-Artuby

GRAND HOTEL BAIN
Village centre
☎ (94) 76 90 06
This 20-room *logis* of the Var, north of Draguignan has been run by the Bain family since 1737, fifty years before the Revolution. The hotel specializes in delicious, copious and traditional cooking, with dishes such as *pâté aux truffes*, and game, and home-made pastries. Menus from F60 to F150. Good wine list. Highly recommended.

04000 Digne

HOTEL DU BOURGOGNE
Ave de Verdon
☎ (92) 31 00 19
A good 2-star *logis* in this pleasant mountain town at the end of the Alpes de Provence railway. 16 rooms and menus from F85 to F250.

LE GRAND PARIS
19 Boulevard Thiers
☎ (93) 31 11 15
M. Ricaud runs a very fine restaurant here with menus from F145 to F320 – not cheap but very good. A good range of wine from the Rhone and Provencal vineyards.

83440 Fayence

MOULIN DE LA CAMANDOULE
Chemin Notre-Dame des Cyprès
☎ (94) 76 00 84
This hotel, run with great precision by Wolf and Shirley Rilla, is just one good reason to visit Fayence, a *village-perché* in the hills behind the coast of the Var, some 40 miles from Nice. The food is excellent, the bedrooms comfortable, there is a pool, and the beautiful town of Fayence is just a walk away. Recommended.

AUBERGE DE LA FONTAINE
Route de Fréjus
☎ (94) 76 07 59
A small *logis* with just seven rooms and a good restaurant with menus priced from F65 to F150. Best to book.

83980 Le Lavandou

HOTEL-RESTAURANT LA RAMADE
16 Rue du Patron Ravello
☎ (94) 71 20 40
A very pleasant *logis* by the beach, with a cheery dining room and good local food. 21 rooms and sensibly priced menus ranging from F72 to F170, with dishes like bouillabaisse, *marmite du pêcheur*, bourride, *aïoli*, langoustines, *plateau de coquillages*. Closed Thursday.

06250 Mougins

RESTAURANT FEU FOLLET
Place Marie
☎ (93) 90 15 78
Mougins has no lack of good restaurants, including the famous Moulin de Mougins, but you will eat very well at this one, with menus priced from F90 to F150. Try the Sisteron lamb and the *magret de canard*. Closed Sunday evening and Monday.

06000 Nice

CHEZ LES PECHEURS
18 Quai des Docks
☎ (93) 89 59 61
Nice is full of good restaurants, with a remarkably fine selection in the Courts Salaya, where a great flower market is held every morning, and the city is well worth a visit. I have chosen to include this restaurant, which serves excellent seafood and other Niçois specialities on menus from F185 to F305 – not the cheapest restaurant in town by any means, but a very good one. Closed Wednesday.

06580 Pegomas

HOTEL LES JASMINS
Quartier du Logis
☎ (93) 42 22 94
A small 1-star *logis* with 14 rooms and menus from F55 to F180. Closed from September to March, but worth a visit in the spring and summer.

83640 Plan d'Aups

HOTEL LOU PEBRE D'AI
Sainte-Baume
St Zacharie
☎ (42) 04 50 42
A Provençal name graces this fine 2-star *logis*, set in a beauty spot below the Sainte Baume mountains, surrounded by a great forest. The restaurant serves award-winning food with both modern and traditional dishes and menus ranging from F95 to F200. 15 rooms. Private, heated pool, tennis, golf, riding – a real hotel. Recommended.

83700 St Raphaël

HOTEL DU DEBARQUEMENT
Route Nationale 98
La Dramont
☎ (94) 82 02 51
The *débarquement* in question was the American landings in the South of France in August 1949, the second D-Day. This *logis* has 16 rooms, and the menus are largely based on fish, with such dishes as *bouillabaisse* and turbot, with stuffed capons just for a change. Many local dishes with good menus. Menus from F67 to F150. Restaurant closed Saturday and Sunday from end of October to beginning of April.

06140 Vence

HOTEL LA ROSERAIE
Ave Henri Giraud
☎ (93) 58 02 20
There are three *logis* in this small hill town. This one has 12 rooms and a notably good F170 menu, matched by a good wine list. Closed January.

05400 Veynes

LE RELAIS DE LA POSTE
35 Rue Berthelot
☎ (95) 57 22 25
A village of the Hautes-Alpes on the Provence-Alpes-Côte d'Azur route, so if you are heading north, stop at M. Marcel's restaurant for the *tarte aux noix*. 12 rooms. Menus from F84 to F247. Restaurant closed January, and Monday in other months. Recommended.

Corsica

20260 Calvi

HOTEL LA CARAVELLE
La Plage
☎ (95) 65 01 21
This beach-front *logis* has 20 rooms and menus from F80 to F150, plus a good selection of Provençal wines.

20126 Evisa

AITONE-HOTEL
Village centre
☎ (95) 26 02 04
Evisa is a pleasant town of the Haute-Corse, set at the end of a road inland from Porto-Ota on the eastern coast. The restaurant serves a mixture of French and Corsican specialities on menus priced from F80 to F120, and a selection of Provençal and Corsican wines. 32 rooms. Closed November and December.

20140 Filitosa

HOTEL LE TORREEN
Village centre
☎ (95) 74 00 91
Most visitors to Corsica make the excursion to Filitosa. This *logis* has 20 rooms and a restaurant serving good food. Menus available from F60.

20213 Fotelli-Plage

HOTEL SAN PELLIGRINO
Castellari-de-Casinea
☎ (95) 36 90 61
This little resort on the east coast of Corsica is much less crowded than the more popular places like Bonifacio, and well worth visiting. This hotel has 54 rooms and a restaurant offering good-value menus from F86 to F150.

20225 Muro

MARE-E-MONTE
Felicito
☎ (95) 61 73 06
You can enjoy the two aspects of Corsica, the sea and the mountains, from this excellent 17-room *logis* near Calvi in the north of the island. Menus from F100 to F150. Closed from October to May.

USEFUL BOOKS

Books abound on the food and wine of France, and a small, select number of titles can be most useful. From all those available I recommend you obtain the following as a basic library, though a wider selection will be found after this list:

The Michelin *Green Guides to France*. Many of these are in English, but all give useful and detailed information on the attractions of the various regions and provinces.

The Michelin *Red Guide*. This annual publication gives a comprehensive list of hotels and restaurants in France. Michelin award rosettes to the better restaurants, and this award sets the bench-mark for French cuisine. The possession of one or more rosettes indicates a good restaurant, though prices will inevitably rise with the number of rosettes awarded.

The *Guide des Hôtels-restaurants, Logis et Auberges de France*. Already mentioned and recommended. Obtainable free, or, by post, in return for a stamped (£1), self-addressed envelope, from the French Government Tourist Office, 178 Piccadilly, London W1V 0AL.

The *Gault-Millau Guide*. This annual publication, most easily purchased in France, lists and describes a wide selection of hotels and restaurants, awarding *toques* (chefs' hats) to the more distinguished. The full descriptions of the food, wine and restaurant ambience in the recommended restaurants can be useful and is often entertaining.

The Pocket Guide to French Food and Wine by Tessa Youell and

George Kimball, published by Xanadu, 1985. A slim book, packed with information on both these subjects, but with lots of detail on local dishes, and therefore very useful in the country districts.

The International Pocket Food Book – and Menu Decoder by Quentin Crew, published by Mitchell Beazley, 1980. This is the book to turn to if you have forgotten that *lotte* is really sea-bass or can't remember if *pissaladière* is something with dandelions or is like a pizza (it's like a pizza). I use my copy all the time.

There are two more I must personally recommend. The first is Don Phillpot's *The Vineyards of France* (Moorland 1987), not least because Don includes all the vineyards open to visitors. The second is Pamela Vandyke Price's *France for the Gourmet Traveller* (Harrap 1988), which goes into the subject of food and wine and how to combine them, in considerable and entertaining detail. Those who seek further enlightenment than I have provided here will find all these books, and those below, useful, and they can add a great deal of enjoyment to travelling and eating in France.

Auvergne & the Massif Central. Rex Grizell. Christopher Helm 1989.
Boulogne – The French Escapade. David Wickers & Deirdre Vine. Seagull Publications 1983.
Burgundy on a Budget. Patrick Delaforce. Mildmay 1987.
The Collins Guide to France. Ed. John Ardagh. Collins-Willow Books 1985.
Encore Travellers' France. Arthur Eperon. Pan 1982.
France à la Carte. Richard Binns. Corgi 1986.
France – For the Independent Traveller. John P. Harris. Macmillan (Papermac) 1987.
La France à Votre Table (The Gastronomic Routes of France). Ed. Le Carrousel Publicité for SOPEXA (Society for the Promotion of Sales of Food and Agricultural Products), France. Published annually in July.
The French Coast. Martin Collins. Moorland 1985 (visitors' guide).
French Country Cooking. Elizabeth David. Penguin 1979.
French Entrée 2: Townsend Thoresen Guide to the French Channel Ports. Patricia Fenn. Quiller Press 1983.
French Entrée 3: Townsend Thoresen Guide to Normandy. Patricia Fenn. Quiller Press 1985.
French Leave 3. Richard Dinns. Corgi 1986.
French Wines 1988/89. Ed. André Vedel. Macdonald Orbis 1988.
Gastronomic Routes of France. Ed. S. Cointat. Le Carrousel Publicité for SOPEXA, Paris.

Guide to Normandy. Robin Neillands. Robert Nicholson 1985.

Le Guide des Vins et des Vignobles de France. Edouard Kressman. Elsevier Séquoia, Paris 1975.

Hidden France. Richard Binns. Corgi 1982.

Off the Beaten track: 'France'. ed. Martin Collins. Moorland 1988.

The Wines & Vineyards of France. Alexis Lichine. Weidenfeld and Nicolson 1979.

Index